CHRIS CLAREMONT

FREDERICK LUIS ALDAMA, SERIES EDITOR

CHRIS CLAREMONT

J. ANDREW DEMAN

UNIVERSITY PRESS OF MISSISSIPPI / JACKSON

The University Press of Mississippi is the scholarly publishing agency of the Mississippi Institutions of Higher Learning: Alcorn State University, Delta State University, Jackson State University, Mississippi State University, Mississippi University for Women, Mississippi Valley State University, University of Mississippi, and University of Southern Mississippi.

www.upress.state.ms.us

The University Press of Mississippi is a member of the Association of University Presses.

Title page portrait by Antony Hare

Any discriminatory or derogatory language or hate speech regarding race, ethnicity, religion, sex, gender, class, national origin, age, or disability that has been retained or appears in elided form is in no way an endorsement of the use of such language outside a scholarly context.

Copyright © 2025 by University Press of Mississippi
All rights reserved
Manufactured in the United States of America

∞

Publisher: University Press of Mississippi, Jackson, USA
Authorised GPSR Safety Representative: Easy Access System Europe - Mustamäe tee 50, 10621 Tallinn, Estonia, gpsr.requests@easproject.com

Library of Congress Cataloging-in-Publication Data

Names: Deman, J. Andrew author
Title: Chris Claremont / J. Andrew Deman.
Description: Jackson : University Press of Mississippi, 2025. | Series: Biographix | Includes bibliographical references and index.
Identifiers: LCCN 2025005543 (print) | LCCN 2025005544 (ebook) | ISBN 9781496859563 hardback | ISBN 9781496859570 trade paperback | ISBN 9781496859587 epub | ISBN 9781496859594 epub | ISBN 9781496859600 pdf | ISBN 9781496859617 pdf
Subjects: LCSH: Claremont, Chris, 1950– | Comics writers—United States—Biography | LCGFT: Biographies
Classification: LCC PN6727.C55 Z57 2025 (print) | LCC PN6727.C55 (ebook) | DDC 741.5/973 [B]—dc23/eng/20250224
LC record available at https://lccn.loc.gov/2025005543
LC ebook record available at https://lccn.loc.gov/2025005544

British Library Cataloging-in-Publication Data available

To Mari and Ari. If I dedicate enough books to you, you'll have to read these comics at some point, right?

CONTENTS

INTRODUCTION 3

CHAPTER ONE:
That Actor/Intern:
Early Life and Beginning of Marvel Career 20

CHAPTER TWO:
Nobody Cared What We Were Doing:
The Cockrum and Byrne Years 28

CHAPTER THREE:
The Long Game: The Smith and Romita Era 52

CHAPTER FOUR:
Mutant Mitosis: The X Spin-Offs 78

CHAPTER FIVE:
Two Infernos:
The Silvestri and Lee Years and the Departure 98

CHAPTER SIX:
Returning Legend:
Subsequent Returns and Other Notable Works 111

CONCLUSION:
Traces Visible to Those Who Know Where to Look:
A Guide to Spotting Claremont's Legacy 122

ACKNOWLEDGMENTS 127

NOTES 129

WORKS CITED 133

INDEX 139

CHRIS CLAREMONT

Introduction

> If O'Neil, McGregor, and Gerber had been Scorsese, Robert Altman, and Francis Ford Coppola, Claremont was Steven Spielberg: the bridge between the fan-favorite auteur and the high-earning superstars of the eighties and nineties.
> —Grant Morrison (177)

In North America, comics production is often divided into two camps: the mainstream and the underground/alternative comics scenes. Though these camps were nowhere near as mutually exclusive as they might have seemed, it is nonetheless fair to say that the vast majority of the comics artists who've been singled out for literary analysis and appreciation have not come from the mainstream.

But then there's Chris Claremont. Even within the narrower sphere of superhero comics (or even just Marvel Comics) Claremont's work has generated the kind of popular appeal that has often eluded authors who are more commonly associated with "cult followings" such as the O'Neils, McGregors, and Gerbers that Morrison mentions. Indeed, like Spielberg, the story of Chris Claremont is the story of a creator who achieved popular success while making a significant artistic contribution to his chosen medium. As comics expert Douglas Wolk notes: "For ten straight years, *The Uncanny X-Men* was the unstoppable behemoth of American mainstream comics both as a commercial enterprise and as art: a fantastically rich, inventive story about the meaning of and value of group identity ... the series' form and cast and setting constantly mutated, sometimes radically, around Claremont's assured, raconteurial voice" (136). This rare double success, however, was not won by playing it safe in the interest of popular appeal. This is an author, after all, who pushed so hard against the status quo that he was effectively fired from writing what was, at the time, the best-selling comic in his industry. Claremont's economic success was noteworthy. Similar to Spielberg in his cultivation of the "blockbuster" film, Claremont elevated his X-Men comic in particular to a must-read franchise that dominated sales charts.

And, like Spielberg again, Claremont innovated. As noted in my previous monograph[1] (but worth repeating), Claremont's milestone accomplishments include

> the first African American superheroine (Cocca 125), the first black superhero team leader (Darowski 78), the first canonically Jewish superhero (Cronin), extensive queer subtext (Fawaz 35), extensive BDSM (bondage, domination, submission, and masochism) imagery (Howe 77), the first superhero team with a strong female roster (Powell 73), the best-selling single-issue comic of all time (Glenday 300), and of course the longest continuous run by a single author in Marvel's history (Powell 6). (Deman, *The Claremont Run* 2)

That all of this was done within mainstream comics and under the microscope of being the best-selling author in the industry at the time is impressive. Thus, the innate question of this volume, "who is Chris Claremont?" gives rise to a second question of simply "how did this guy do this?" Happily, for the purposes of this volume, those two questions are, in essence, the same. And so we can begin our study.

First, a disclaimer of sorts: as with any study of a creator in the collaborative medium of comics, we have to note that Chris Claremont, as he's known to the world, is the product of more individuals than just Chris Claremont, the British kid hired to work at Marvel. Rather, Claremont is an author who succeeds in a collaborative medium in large part due to the strength of his collaborators. Claremont himself is deeply conscious of this and of the many voices that helped to inflect and inform his own as an author. In a 1988 essay, Claremont describes the appeal of the collaborative storytelling method of comics in contrast to the (usually more venerated) idea of a single creative voice:

> One of the absolute joys of comics—as both a profession and an art form—is that it allows you to work in collaboration with other people. There's a school of thought which says that the creative process is best served when there is only a single artistic mind involved from start to finish—the same person writing and pencilling and inking a story, giving it an absolute coherence of vision. There's something to be said for that. But there is also something to be said for the collaborative effort. A synthesis of the talents and creative instincts of a writer, a penciller and an editor, wherein what emerges may not be the pristine product of a single mind but may instead—when all the elements click—be a whole which is far greater than the sum of its parts. (Introduction to *Captain Britain*, 7)

Thus, "Chris Claremont" as acclaimed author might be said to be a synthesis of talents rather than an individual auteur.

This perspective is important to keep in mind when studying Claremont's body of work. Hired by Stan Lee, mentored by Roy Thomas, and inheriting works developed by Jack Kirby, Arnold Drake, Neal Adams, and Len Wein (all Will Eisner Award Hall of Fame inductees), Claremont was positioned to succeed. This positionality was greatly enhanced through his direct collaborators, who include some of the finest in the industry: Archie Goodwin, Barry Windsor-Smith, Frank Miller and John Buscema (all inductees as well). We can add to that list noteworthy names such as Dave Cockrum, Louise Simonson, John Romita Jr., Ann Nocenti, Glynnis Oliver, Tom Orzechowski, Jim Shooter, Marc Silvestri, Arthur Adams, George Pérez, Jim Lee, Walt Simonson, Salvador Larroca, and, of course, John Byrne. Simply put, Claremont has spent his entire career surrounded by some of the finest creators in his field. That privilege has to be acknowledged and contextualized, yet what Chris Claremont did within his privileged position remains impressive in its own right.

In many circles, Claremont is known for some potentially negative quirks: excess wordiness (Wolk 146), overreliance on "a dark side to human identity which might consume or unbalance the rational, stable self" (Booy 12), and, relatedly, stories about mind control (Wolk 145). To his editors, he was fiercely protective of his characters and titles (Simonson qtd. in DeFalco 139, Jim Shooter qtd. in "Jim Shooter" n.p.). To his collaborators, he was too expansive in his plot submissions (Silvestri qtd. in DeFalco 161, Byrne qtd. in DeFalco 101) or even humorless in the severity with which he approached his work (Cockrum qtd. in DeFalco 95). As I will demonstrate, however, these quirks and complaints can just as easily be perceived as aspects of the things that make Claremont an important author in comics history.

First and foremost, Claremont (trained as a method actor) brought to the world of comics a commitment to character depth that transcended certain expectations of the medium and genre that he found himself working in. This would lead to what Marvel historian Sean Howe calls "the soapiest saga ever put forth by the House of Ideas, filled with agonized romances, self-confidence crises, lectures on morality, psychic scars, and worrying" (210). Claremont himself describes his approach to character as follows:

> That to me is storytelling. Instead of giving readers the cliché of "fight fight fight" it's like, "What's going on beneath the hood, what's going on with Spider-Man, or his relationship with MJ?" The Fantastic Four trying to keep themselves from going broke.... That to me is the cool stuff. You know, we all know, at least in the days of the Comics Code, the heroes will win every time. But there's a lot more that can go on beneath the surface during the fight, after the fight, that readers might find interesting. And, as a writer, that's the ocean I want to fish in. And I figure, egotistically, if I'm having fun—then maybe readers are too. ("I'm Chris Claremont" n.p.)

This approach has been lauded by both industry insiders and comics scholars. In a 1993 essay, Stan Lee, the cocreator of X-Men comics, provides his personal perspective on Claremont's Uncanny X-Men work, noting that "their adventures reflect real life (although a wilder life than most of us will ever experience!) . . . though it sounds like a real-life contradiction in terms, perhaps the main appeal of the colorful, outrageous, outlandish, bigger-than-life, fantasy-filled X-Men is their sheer and total realism!" (Lee 378). Others, such as scholar Douglas Wolk, interpret Claremont's style as hyperbolic rather than realistic, and to pointed effect: "Of course his work is emotionally oversized—that's the whole idea. (The same could be said of Freddie Mercury or Maria Callas or Otis Redding)" (147).

To this purpose of grounded emotional hyperbole (an apt if somewhat paradoxical description of Claremont's style), one of the most prominent characterization strategies employed by Claremont for his characters (along with torturing them emotionally) is filling them with an intense sense of self-doubt with accompanying self-questioning that plays out in the thought bubbles or narrative captions. This approach has something of a tradition at Marvel. Self-doubting characters can be seen clearly in the original Fantastic Four comics but were brought to bold new heights by Spider-Man stories in the same era. Claremont's protagonists operate in a similar way—constantly expressing a lack of interior confidence and routinely questioning their own capacity to even function as superheroes. Whole pages are filled, at times, with self-condemning internal monologues in the vein of *Hamlet*. With self-doubt in play, the narrative becomes one of complex self-realization in which characters overcome conflicts that are self-imposed more often than external. In this, the real battle is often a psychodrama in which the protagonist can serve as their own antagonist, even to the extreme (at times) of self-destructive behaviors.

An extreme example of this would be the significant number of Claremont superheroes suffering from both active and passive suicidal ideation, a fairly rare occurrence for comics of the time.

His portrayal of a physically, emotionally, and spiritually exhausted Wolverine character in the late 1980s is referenced as a death wish by multiple characters on multiple occasions. In the "Brood Saga" storyline that transpires across *Uncanny X-Men* (or *UXM* for short) #161–67, his Storm character is placed in a position where she, too, actively contemplates suicide, including extended thought bubbles exploring the concept. In that same character's "Lifedeath" story a few years later, Storm is again contemplating killing herself. Rogue—when particularly strained by the struggle to disambiguate her consciousness from Carol Danvers—directly expresses a desire to die ("Madness"). Claremont's Madelyne Pryor character has to be literally talked down from jumping off a cliff at one point ("Omens and Portents"). In the X-Men spin-off, *Excalibur*, Captain Britain expresses suicidal thoughts on multiple occasions. Then, *Classic X-Men* #11 features a backup story where Claremont portrays a writer (who is an obvious surrogate for Claremont himself) contemplating suicide before being saved—essentially—by meeting Storm, though for how long that will last is left unclear ("Hope"). Claremont characters are, more often than not, hanging on by a thread, and this can lend them a vulnerability that is both intimate and relatable.

Similarly, his characters are also frequently made to grapple with fear and anxiety beyond the norm for superheroes. Arguably, the very concept of the superhero (and the power fantasy it projects) is built around heroic, unflappable, and sometimes irrational bravery; yet Claremont routinely populates his world with characters who are quite capable of genuinely debilitating terror, such as with Storm's struggle with claustrophobia. Famously, Wolverine has a panic attack in an issue of *Uncanny X-Men* ("The Action of the Tiger"). Then, in the wake of the death of the superheroine Phoenix and the groundbreaking establishment of superhero mortality through said death,[2] fears become a bit more directly rational, with characters like Kitty Pryde providing a mouthpiece for considerations of apprehension and anxiety in the face of danger. When Claremont writes Justice League ("The Tenth Circle"), his Superman is immediately rendered vulnerable by magic. All combined, Claremont's characters are animated by big emotions, big internal struggles, and a notable departure from the traditional broad heroic paradigm as well as an advanced evolution of the specific Marvel paradigm of self-doubting heroes.

Importantly, this depth that Claremont afforded his characters was not limited to those identifying as male, and the author has earned a particular reputation for his portrayal of women. This is no accident, but, according to Claremont himself, a conscious undertaking. He notes:

> Women tend to get very short shrift in comics. They are either portrayed as wallflowers or as super-macho insensitive men with different body forms, who almost invariably feel guilty about their lack of femininity. And it's always seemed to me that, why does this have to be exclusive? Can you not have a woman who is ruthless and capable and courageous and articulate and intelligent and all the other buzzwords—heroic when the need arises, and yet feminine and gentle and compassionate, at others? (qtd. in Sanderson 23–24)

The success of Claremont's undertaking is open to interpretation[3] but the first stage of representation is simple existence/presence, and, as scholar Sam Langsdale notes, "Female-led superhero comics, with diverse casts of characters that cultivate inclusive feminist storytelling and art, exist on the margins of the US mainstream super-hero genre" (2). Yet Claremont's writing stands out for his creation of a female-led superhero comic with a diverse cast of characters. The art is perhaps outside of his scope, but feminist storytelling, as I will demonstrate, is very much within it.

Speaking quite directly, Claremont's contributions to the Marvel canon of great female characters is evident, creating or cocreating Kitty Pryde, Rogue, Psylocke, Mystique, Emma Frost, Jubilee, Valeria Richards, Karima Shipandar, Moira MacTaggert, Wolfsbane, Moonstar, Karma, while developing other characters such as Storm, Ms. Marvel, Magik, Colleen Wing, Misty Knight, Black Widow, and innumerable others.

In developing his superheroines, Claremont was operating against the grain of an industry that was out of touch with the times in the eyes of scholar Carol Cooper:

> When Wein turned scripting of the resurrected X-Men title over to Claremont in the mid-'70s, there were no female team leaders in any superhero comic. Despite Golda Meir, Indira Gandhi and ultimately Margaret Thatcher, the decision-makers in mainstream comics didn't seem ready to portray women running the show. Claremont changed all that. First, he increased the abilities and strengths of all his female characters. He gave them complex motivations and more shrewd situational ethics. Then, and perhaps most uniquely, he imbued his female heroines with traits prototypically associated with ancient goddess traditions. (195)

Thus, it can be argued (as Cooper does) that Claremont altered the patterns by which women were commonly portrayed in Marvel Comics. This argument is articulated in much greater depth in my Eisner-winning volume, *The Claremont Run: Subverting Gender in the X-Men*.

Furthermore, Claremont's progressive approach to gender representation was, arguably, matched by his equally progressive (though highly subversive due to censorship issues of the time) approach to queer representation. As Wolk notes, "LGBTQ readers have embraced *X-Men* like few other comics" (148). Claremont is quite open about his cultivation of queer representation, even expressing some bitterness with how his queer characters have been misperceived or even straightwashed. "Actually, I'm pissed with everything that's being done today that Dave and I or John and I or Paul and I did forty years ago. It took years for anyone to notice why Raven and Irene live together in the same house. What could that be, I haven't a clue?" (personal interview 2). Claremont littered his works with queer subtext, creating implicit representations of characters outside of the heterosexual norm that so dominated mainstream culture of the time.

Important recent works of comics scholarship have taken notice. In his own Eisner-winning book *The New Mutants: Superheroes and the Radical Imagination of American Comics*, Ramzi Fawaz declares that X-Men (under Claremont) "articulated mutation to the radical critiques of identity promulgated by the cultures of women's and gay liberation" (145). Fawaz (with Scott Darieck) would also later describe the "alternative mutant kinships" of superhero stories as "the epitome of queer world making" (197). In each of these arguments, Fawaz's point is that the fundamental setup of X-Men comics—the found family of persecuted outcasts, is innately queer. The term that Fawaz uses is "queer mutanty."

This reading is supported by scholar Carolyn Cocca. In her own Eisner Award–winning monograph, *Superwomen: Gender, Power, and Representation*, Cocca identifies the atypical "found family" dynamic of X-Men as a key component of what made the series special. "One of the strengths of the X-Men universe is in its queer families: its diverse characters who are not related through a 'traditional' and nuclear patriarchal structure, but rather, who choose each other as family based on mutual love and support" (129). For Cocca, this separation from traditional (and heteronormative) family units allows Claremont's X-Men to explore a broader spectrum of relationships outside the usual brothers-in-arms or romance triangles that had historically formed the go-to relationships for many mainstream comics authors.

Adding depth to Claremont's portrayal of the found family dynamic is a parallel portrayal of fractured biological families in much of the author's work. Character arcs built around reconciliation with parents are extensive in Claremont's writing and feature prominently in the stories of major superhero characters such as Iron Fist, Cyclops, Rogue, Storm, Wolverine, Nightcrawler, Rachel Summers, and Valeria Richards. These arcs consistently explore themes of familial estrangement and the emotional fallout that results while building tension toward a possible reconciliation and even sometimes resolving with an actual reconciliation and the catharsis it can produce. These narratives further foreground the concept of found family (again, a key aspect of Fawaz's exploration of queer mutanity), with role model characters quite often fulfilling a substitute parental role for an estranged child. The point is that Claremont is routinely building narrative tension and character development out of a longing for parental reconciliation that may have universal symbolic resonance (who doesn't crave their parents love and approval?) but with specific resonance for a disproportionate number of queer readers.

Claremont's work has also garnered an extensive following in the trans community, in large part due to this same exploration of socially maligned bodies within a found family dynamic. As mentioned in Mady G and Jules Zuckerberg's *A Quick & Easy Guide to Queer & Trans Identities*, "Some (not all) non-binary people feel some kind of connection with nonhuman characters because they feel those things are 'less gendered' than a human body. For this reason, those kinds of non-binary people particularly enjoy things like aliens, robots and other non-human representations" (2). Being nonhuman is, of course, a defining attribute of most of Claremont's characters due to the nature of the superhero genre—an attribute that is constantly reiterated in his works through the thematic exploration of the prejudices these characters encounter.

This portrayal of socially unaccepted mutant/alien/superpowered bodies can be seen to create a unique resonance and point of identification for trans readers through said body's existence outside of established norms and for the hostility with which those bodies are often (but not always) met. This might be approached with the concept of the "monstrous" body, a term appropriated and recontextualized for its radical potentials in the works of Donna Haraway and Judith Butler, who both speak to the emancipatory potential of such bodies. As scholar Jolene Zigarovich describes, "For Butler, 'monster' functions in a space where 'manhood' and 'femininity' meet." Haraway, meanwhile, speaks to the utopian dream of a "monstrous world without gender" in her famous Cyborg Manifesto (181).

The "monstrous" mutant body has actually been very well discussed in scholarship on X-Men, perhaps most notably in Scott Bukatman's *Matters of Gravity*, which describes X-bodies as constantly articulating a metaphorical (or literal) monstrosity (49). Some characters are visibly labeled monsters while others live in fear of monstrous eruptions of their powers and others still are deemed monstrous just for being labeled "mutant." Bukatman's main point is vulnerability: by existing outside of arbitrary bodily norms, society "hates and fears" the X-Men, and that can be a poignant/potent allegory for trans readers. We can even see some complex surfacings of this, such as in Harvard professor Stephanie Burt's poem "Prayer for Werewolves," which uses Claremont's Wolfsbane character to explore, according to Burt, "trans fears of seeming monstrous, of social rejection, of finding love nowhere because our bodies don't fit, fears that can follow trans people both before and after coming out, before and after social or medical transition" (personal interview).

Even perceived from a more generalist perspective, scholars have spoken to the importance of broad representational politics in Claremont's work. In a selected chapter for *Comics Studies: A Guidebook* covering the very broad subject of "Superheroes," scholar Marc Singer provides an account for Claremont's use of representational metaphor in his X-Men stories: "The X-Men were depicted as objects of fear, prejudice, and oppression, leading readers to interpret them as free-floating metaphors for African American, gays, Jews, and other marginalized groups—not to mention adolescents, particularly those outcasts who read comic books. Turning his mutant heroes into a malleable allegory, Claremont created a powerful vehicle for reader identification by conflating a conditional social ostracism with systematic and institutional oppression" (218). Thus Claremont's work can be seen to be quite capable of speaking to a wide swathe of marginalized groups, including those that were not even on the writer's radar.

Relatedly, we should also note Claremont's interest in exploring complex intersectional identities over simple typologies. The concept of self-definition in resistance to external forces is one of the most pervasive thematic threads throughout Claremont's work—the idea that we, as individuals, get to define ourselves, even when pressured to conform to preexisting expectations. As most people know, the revamped X-Men were specifically created to attract an international market, using stereotypical characters linked to different ethnicities. But Claremont complicates that almost immediately upon coming onto the book. He complicates the African character Storm by giving her an American heritage and a pluralistic experience of different African nations. Later he portrays the Cheyenne character Forge as an Indigenous man living outside of tribal culture and ideologies. Toward the end of his first run on X-Men, he brings in Jubilee, an Asian American experiencing racism from both sides. Each of these characters, and many others, defy the simplicity of stereotype in ways that can be seen to destabilize established identity barriers.

Then there's more abstract forms of resistance to definition such as Jean Grey refusing her destiny, refusing an enforced maternal role, refusing gender-based hierarchies, all while actively contemplating the impact these expectations have on her sense of individual agency. Wolverine does something similar, refusing the perfect killing machine role that he was born to and cultivated toward by a wide number of forces. He refuses them all and pursues, despite incredible difficulty, self-definition. Cyclops takes it one step further, refusing even the reader's expectations for him. He rejects his presumed obligation to live and die for Xavier's dream, deciding instead to cultivate his own existence outside of both his mentor's vision and (metatextually) that of the reader as well. In a world where superheroes often represent values of duty and obligation, Claremont's work actively teaches all readers that other people's expectations for us are constructs and that we have the right to (perhaps heroically) define ourselves.

Despite all of these representational contributions, we are still left with something of an elephant in the room to talk about with Claremont: what about his much-discussed portrayal of kink in comics? It's a delicate subject and requires some unpacking, but saying that Claremont's X-Men employs BDSM symbolism is kind of like saying that Iron Man comics employ themes of the military-industrial complex. It's pretty obvious. But where that military-industrial complex is an openly discussed, easily broached subject for academic inquiry, BDSM symbolism is not, for a variety of reasons pertaining to Western culture's infamous attitude's about discussing sexuality.

The first thing to note in laying a groundwork here is that these sexual practices have some intriguing intersections with established narrative practices of the superhero genre, which often features bondage as a form of restraint, dominance and submission as elements of conflict, and antagonists defined through practices of sadism that often result in masochistic spectacles of heroic suffering. This overlap means that you're going to get a lot of false positives when you go looking for BDSM symbols in a superhero comic, but it also gives creators plausible deniability with censors when they do directly and intentionally include those symbols in their work, thus empowering the practice in counterintuitive ways.

Fortunately for us, Claremont's use of BDSM symbolism goes way beyond plausible deniability. The obvious evidence here begins with the Hellfire Club from *X-Men* comics (figure 1), Claremont's most famous BDSM symbol (though by no means his only one). Inspired by an episode of the *Avengers* TV series, Claremont and Byrne's Hellfire Club gathered together a number of forms of domination—class, gender, species, and heritage—and intersected them with highly sexualized attire and practices of bondage and sadism. The Hellfire Club also establishes a curious and paradoxical tonal issue in that Claremont quite consistently villain codes his sadist/dom characters. The characters who exhibit the BDSM symbols aren't usually the good guys. We need to note, however, that

Figure 1. The Hellfire Club is revealed in "And Hellfire Is Their Name" (*Uncanny X-Men*, vol. 1, no. 132). John Byrne, penciller.

Claremont also draws forward discussions of consent, featuring them prominently in things like Professor Xavier's ideals about the ethics of telepathy, ideals that, yes, he breaks a lot but at least those conversations are happening and those values espoused. They also come forward in key scenes of BDSM symbolism, such as Callisto's abduction of Angel and Storm's reflection on the distinction between desire and love ("Dancin' in the Dark").

All of this leaves us with more questions than answers, but that's always a good start to an academic inquiry:

- Does the juxtaposition of sexualized characters and sadistic intent make them somehow both more threatening and more appealing simultaneously?

- Does Claremont use scenes of accidental undress a lot to humiliate his characters?

- Is Rogue's symbolic representation of restraint in the form of avoiding all touch somehow a source of sexual tension?

- Do Wolverine's sadistic elements make him more sexually appealing in general?

- How does BDSM imagery juxtapose Ms. Marvel's role as a symbol of second-wave feminism?

These questions are important and the answers may be complex, paradoxical, or subjective. Consider, for contrast, Noah Berlatsky's account of bondage imagery in Wonder Woman comics (a character Claremont would go on to write in the course of his career): "Though some critics and feminists see fetishized bondage as disempowering to women, I point out that representations of disempowerment are popular in women's genre literature such as the romance and the gothic. Images of disempowerment, then, may be popular with women because they mirror women's actual disempowerment" (13). Similarly put, Claremont's portrayal of BDSM imagery may have been appealing to female readers as often as (or more often than) it was offensive. Alternately, it might have been both.

Nonetheless, in all of these questions and the multivalent answers they might generate, we can see how the BDSM symbolism informs the narrative tension, character dynamics, and queer sensibility of X-Men comics. Our culture still doesn't really want us to talk about BDSM, but if we want to understand the comics of Chris Claremont, we're going to have to.

The final piece of legacy to track throughout this text is Claremont's important cultivation of long-form storytelling structures in Marvel Comics (and beyond). Claremont maintains that his sixteen-year run on *Uncanny X-Men* (the necessary focus of this volume) is a single cohesive story (personal interview 2). Due to the sheer size and scale of that, "Appreciating the long-form storytelling of Claremont is out of the box for most of us taught to appreciate literature in college, great masterworks usually in one volume" (Klock 3). Thus, his most famous work is perhaps too large to fit within the infrastructure of literary analysis and appreciation.

One of the earliest strategies we can identify toward this unusual scale of storytelling is his practice of chaining together conflicts in direct succession in order to form a (moderately) continuous narrative. As an example, beginning in "Mindgames" from *Uncanny X-Men* #111, the X-Men are ambushed and brainwashed by Mesmero. In typical heroic fashion, they are able to break Mesmero's spell and confront him . . . only to find themselves in the clutches of Magneto. Magneto easily defeats them and imprisons them in his volcano lair. In typical heroic fashion, they escape, defeat Magneto in combat and narrowly escape the erupting Volcano . . . only to find themselves in the Savage Land, where they are ambushed by Sauron. In typical heroic fashion, they defeat the were-pterosaur and bring him back to his human identity, Dr. Karl Lykos . . . only to become embroiled in a broader conflict with the fate of the Savage Land at stake. In typical heroic fashion, they engage with Zaladane and Garrok, defeating their cult and escaping back to the surface . . . only to land in Japan, where allies Sunfire, Misty Knight, and Colleen Wing recruit the X-Men for their assistance in defeating Moses Magnum. In typical heroic fashion, they storm Magnum's lair to destroy his earthquake machine and save Japan before finally flying homeward . . . only to be ambushed by Alpha Flight in a misguided attempt by the Canadian government to reclaim Wolverine to lead their shadowy special forces unit. In typical heroic fashion, they engage with Alpha Flight and save the city of Calgary from an out-of-control blizzard. And then—and only then—the X-Men make it to home base, finally resetting to status quo from their base of operations (the X-Mansion) twelve issues later. Along the way, the characters all undergo individual character arcs that overlap the separation of events and create a bit of broader cohesion.

Nor was this strategy limited to X-Men. We can identify similar patterns in his runs on *Iron Fist, Excalibur, Ms. Marvel,* and *Fantastic Four*. The question then becomes, were these discrete story arcs or one continuous *Odyssey*-like macrostory? The answer depends on the level of engagement of the reader (casual vs. devotee). The stories reward either approach and that's kind of the point: by appealing to both the norm (the presumed casual readership) AND the emerging devotee market (empowered by the newly forming comics store culture), Claremont was/is able to transition toward long-continuity storytelling at a time when it was still atypical for a comic to assume a reader had even read the previous issue in a series. This balance in Claremont's work would shift throughout his run (as chronicled in the chapters ahead), with the author putting more and more weight into the devotee presumption and subsequently also putting more and more complexity into his own narrative.

In summation, then: depth of character, breakthroughs in progressive representation, and advancing the cause of long-form storytelling in the comics medium—these are the cornerstone arguments that this book makes in support of Claremont's implicit application to comics posterity. The pages ahead are divided loosely by chronology but also by subject text. The focus will, of course, be on his unprecedented sixteen-year run as author of *Uncanny X-Men* comics, the story that Claremont is most famously associated with, but that same critical lens will be applied to other much-loved Claremont runs and stories as well as some more obscure works, all of this with the overarching goal of exploring how one author brought auteur innovation to the Marvel mainstream with a scale of influence that only a popular platform could provide. Simply put, what Claremont did should not have worked, and figuring out how it did requires a deep, deep dive into the life, world, and works of Chris Claremont.

CHAPTER ONE

That Actor/Intern

Early Life and Beginning of Marvel Career

> We were just a bunch of punk kids working in the back end of Magazine Management. Nobody bought comics. It was a dying industry, and we knew it. Nobody cared. We were just there to have fun.
> —Chris Claremont (qtd. in Howe 168)

Chris Claremont was born in London in 1950 to an internist and his wife, a caterer. At the age of three, he immigrated to the United States and was raised, primarily, on Long Island, just a ninety-minute drive from the office of Marvel Comics, where he would one day undertake the longest single-author tenure on a comics title, surpassing even Stan Lee in that regard.

Claremont's mother worked for the British Air Force in WWII and later became a pilot. Her influence manifests in Claremont's work in both specific and abstract ways. For one thing, Claremont's works feature a significant number of women pilots, including a trilogy of novels commonly referred to as "The Nicole Shea" series (after star pilot Lieutenant Nicole Shea). More abstractly, we also see the impact of Claremont's mother reflected in the empowering joy of flying that Claremont depicts with the Storm character, as well as other female flyers, such as Rogue and Phoenix. Claremont also cultivated the military aviatrix background of Ms. Marvel, an important gender-nonconforming thread that would later be picked up by Kelley Sue DeConnick in her *Captain Marvel* run and, eventually, the feature film of the same name. Thus, we can see attributes of Claremont's mother in some of the most famous and compelling superheroines that Marvel has ever produced.

It is perhaps safe to say as well that Claremont's general respect and admiration for his mother informed his commitment to progressive representations of women in general. As noted by scholars such as Scott Bukatman (65) and Carol Cooper (195), pre-Claremont Marvel heroines tended to have stand-and-pose powers such as telepathy, telekinesis, and force fields. Claremont pushed against this trend with heroines who often got their hands dirty with powers such as energy blasts, superstrength, and enhanced martial artistry (in addition to the aforementioned power of flight). For both Bukatman and Cooper, this decision was an important step toward more progressive representations of female characters in Marvel Comics.

Claremont's relationship to his father is perhaps less approachable, but paternal conflict is a particularly common theme in Claremont's writing. For example, in describing his approach to the Rachel Summers character from *Uncanny X-Men* and *Excalibur*, the author writes, "How would *you* feel if you suddenly learned that the dad you loved had other children you never knew about? Some of us—me included—have to deal with that in our real lives. Here you can see, for better or ill, how I dealt with that on the page" ("A Lost Soul" 312). This passage, of course, reveals not just that Claremont had some emotional turmoil in his relationship with his father but also that he used his creative writing as an outlet for exploring those conflicts, thus again transposing aspects of a parent to his fictional universes.

On the subject of religion, Claremont's faith and relationship to said faith is complicated. He was Jewish on his mother's side and recounts in an essay how "In University, I had spent time in Israel working on a kibbutz, many of whose members were survivors of the Holocaust. This became the defining experience of my life" ("No Straw Dogs Here" 8). Said experience manifests in Claremont's work in a number of ways: his cocreation of Marvel's first canonical Jewish superhero, Kitty Pryde; the cultivation of a sympathetic portrayal of villain character Magneto as a Holocaust survivor; and, in general, Claremont's use of Jewish symbols in his mapping of the "mutant metaphor" in X-Men comics, including the portrayal of mutant concentration camps. In *Disguised as Clark Kent: Jews, Comics, and the Creation of the Superhero*, Danny Fingeroth credits Claremont with taking the Jewish symbols of X-Men comics from subtext to text: "What Lee and Kirby had hinted at became explicit" (121).

Judaism was not the only religion to play a pivotal role in Claremont's work, however. The other notable influence in play is Wicca, a badly misunderstood faith that is often shrouded in secrecy and obscured by popular myths about witchcraft. Claremont has not been forthcoming about this aspect of his life (nor should he have to be), but his personal records reveal his participation in Wicca conferences and gatherings in the early 1980s (Claremont Papers), and his first wife, Bonnie Wilford, has been identified as a Wiccan high priestess known as Graymalkin,[1] with Marvel historian Sean Howe noting, "Claremont began drawing on his own interest in the occult and religion" and "In early 1977, Claremont married Bonnie Wilford, a Gardnerian Wiccan; according to one friend, they were 'quite active in the New York City demimonde'" (197). When I asked Claremont in an interview why there were so many Wiccan themes in his work, his response was simply that "a lady I was with at the time was in it" (personal interview 2). Gardnerian Wicca is a traditional branch of British Wicca that is known for operating in secrecy (Valiente). The religion is duotheistic, with worship spread between the horned god and the mother goddess. Aspects of the faith can be seen in a wide number of Claremont characters, including Storm, Jean, Spiral, Magik, Margali, Amanda Sefton, Dr. Strange, Selene, the Goblin Queen, and many more, though articulating the full extent of Wicca themes in Claremont's work is beyond the scope of this project.

In terms of education, Claremont attended Bard College, a small, private, liberal arts college in Red Hook overlooking the

Hudson. The school traces its history back to 1860 and was founded by the grandson of George Washington's personal physician. Claremont describes the school as follows: "[They had a] 400-student cohort. Very left-wing, avant-garde, holding on by our fingernails, trying not to go broke. And yet some of the most extraordinary faculty.[2] Hannah Arendt's husband taught there my first year. We had a lot of expat German theorists. It was a place of remarkable opportunities. Everything, it seemed, was improvised. It was fun" (personal interview 2). His time there wasn't all fun, however, as he notes in one introductory paper that he contemplated suicide while there at one point. "Happened in college, dead of winter, sophomore year, about as bleak and depressing a time as can be imagined. But I didn't act on it. Not sure now I even took it seriously" ("Introduction" from *New Mutants Omnibus* vol. 2). Nonetheless, Claremont's work frequently explores the concept of suicidal ideation, as discussed in the introduction.

Claremont's education at Bard also came with some twists and turns that eventually led him to a career at Marvel Comics after he took a between-term job as a gopher in the Marvel offices:

> My initial academic training was in political theory. I thought, you know, go to work and help save the world back in the day—except that I really wanted to try acting, and the only way I could get into a class was to declare an acting major, and graduate 4 years later with a degree in acting. I don't know if you've ever tried to get a job with a degree in acting—along the way I would always write. It was fun, it was something I did. And then when I was just out of high school, I sold my first short story, and then I sold another, and then Marvel bought a story, and another, and another—and then oddly enough I got the X-Men and then 5 years later I realized I wasn't acting any more, I was writing. ("I'm Chris Claremont")

Though Claremont's career was defined by his avocation more than his education, it is safe to say that his training at Bard informed the political philosophy of his work as well as his method approach to writing. As Alec Foege of New York Magazine notes, "Inspired by his acting, he took the Method approach to fleshing out his superheroes. 'What are their goals in life?' he says. 'Who does the dishes? What kind of music do they listen to? . . . See what I mean about subtext and the id writing the books for you?'"

As Claremont notes, he was brought into Marvel by Stan Lee himself and overseen by the comics legend during his early years in the Marvel bullpen. "I was hired by Stan. He had three rules: don't be late, don't be a pain in my ass, do good work. And the joke was if you could do two out of three you could keep your job" (personal interview 2). Claremont's first author credit is for a plot assist on *Uncanny X-Men* #59 in 1969 (Thomas). The mutant-hunting robot villains, the Sentinels, were battling the X-Men again and Claremont contributed a way for the X-Man Cyclops to defeat them by convincing them that the sun was the source of all mutation and that the killer robots should therefore attack the sun (of course, destroying themselves in the process). Though slight in application, it is perhaps momentous that Claremont's first writing for Marvel Comics would be within the franchise that he would later define and that would define his life's work in return.

Throughout the early 1970s, Claremont was a fixture of the Marvel Bullpen as an assistant and as a writer (primarily a fill-in—a job that gave him the opportunity to have a turn with the majority of Marvel's iconic roster of superheroes at one point or another). His first truly notable work, arguably, was the high-concept *War Is Hell* comic that he wrote for Marvel from 1974–1975 with help on plots from Tony Isabella. The series tells the story of the morally ambiguous character John Kowalski, who was killed during Germany's invasion of Poland and now finds himself in a form of purgatory in which Death forces him to relive the last moments of various war casualties as a sort of penance. Though the series was canceled after just seven Claremont-penned issues, it nonetheless provided an ideal showcase for the author's penchant for introspective characters and surreal melodrama. It was an ambitious title that provides a glimpse of Claremont's raw talent and outside-the-box approach to writing.

The year 1975 marks the beginning of Claremont's most notable assignment for Marvel: *Uncanny X-Men*. But given the centrality of that franchise on Claremont's contribution to comics as a whole, I'll defer my discussion of that work to the next chapter (and subsequent chapters) in order to here highlight some of Claremont's other noteworthy Marvel work.

In 1975 Claremont tackled Marvel's *Iron Fist*, undertaking a highly regarded run that, had he stayed on a bit longer, might have been equally famous to his work on *X-Men*. His fifteen-issue *Iron Fist* run features, among other things, the debut of the villain Sabretooth, the cultivation of strong women of color in Colleen Wing and Misty Knight,[3] a pre-X-Men partnership with penciller John Byrne, and some compelling long-continuity storytelling that moves away from the episodic standards of the time.

In 1976, Claremont, having been born in Britain, was tasked with launching a British superhero called Captain Britain for Marvel UK with artwork by Herb Trimpe, who Claremont credits as a lifelong friend from his first day at Marvel (introduction to *Marvel Universe by Chris Claremont*, 5). Unfortunately, the series struggled to find an audience, and Claremont left after ten issues. Later revivals of the hero would, however, provide a major platform for the emerging talents of Alan Moore, Jamie Delano, and Alan Davis, who all cultivated the franchise to new heights that Claremont would then build on himself in the pages of various X-Men comics titles.

In 1977, Claremont was tasked with revitalizing *Ms. Marvel*. Though his run would lay important groundwork for the character that is still being built on today, it wasn't enough to find an audience, and the series was eventually canceled after twenty-three issues. The series nonetheless allowed Claremont to introduce the villain character Mystique and, more importantly, to experiment quite directly with a superempowered female character: "That was what I tried to do with Ms. Marvel. I tried to create a character who had all the attributes that made her a top-secret agent yet at the same time was a compassionate, warm, humorous, witty, intelligent, attractive woman" (qtd. in Sanderson 23). Claremont would also later write an important reparative Ms. Marvel story in the pages of *Avengers Annual* #10 ("By Friends—Betrayed!") after an Avengers storyline subjected the character to sexual violence. As Howe recounts, "Chris Claremont, who had invested two years of toil and tears and screaming with editors to transform Ms. Marvel into a respectable character, only to see her cosmically roofied and whisked away to a literal Limbo, was aghast" (Howe 229). His defenses of Carol Danvers reflect once again his commitment to strong female characters in comics.

In 1982, operating outside of the mainstream Marvel continuity, Claremont's creator-owned project *Marada the She-Wolf* debuted. *Marada* was originally devised as a *Red Sonja* project but was modified to be an original story outside of Robert E. Howard's Hyboria due to conflicts with the soon-to-be-released *Red Sonja* film. *Marada*'s publishing history is complicated, but the result has been a cult following. Claremont cocreated the project with John Bolton, who would go on to illustrate the *Classic X-Men* back-up stories discussed in a later chapter. The format here is more prestigious, however, with Bolton given more time and space to cultivate his artwork. The story also features a wide number of tropes familiar to Claremont's readers. Most notably, it centers on a strong, independent female protagonist operating outside of traditional gender roles and just being generally badass.

Following in the footsteps of *Marada the She-Wolf*, Claremont's second pairing with artist John Bolton resulted in *The Black Dragon*, a six-part fantasy series published by Epic Comics in 1985. Where *Marada* offered a Hyborian-style backdrop, *The Black Dragon* takes place in crusade era England and draws in key political and religious conflicts of the time, such as Norman/Saxon and Christian/Pagan. The series is dripping in British mythology and history, thus contrasting effectively with Claremont's later work with Alan Davis on the series *Excalibur*, which takes a similar perspective on British culture (though contemporary rather than historical). *Black Dragon* also incorporates a lot of the faerie realm (including the "bright lady" deity that we see in other Claremont works). Additionally, as with *Marada*, seeing Claremont take his sexual symbolism into an R-rated venue with no Comics Code censorship provides an interesting study of his usual tropes and patterns when it comes to sexuality in his writing. *Black Dragon* features a very literal take on Claremont's frequent sexualization of superpowers with a public Dionysian sexual ritual specifically triggering a demonic transformation. The ritual is described in base terms and contrasts with the impact of love in resolving the conflict and restoring the characters to a state of innocence in the end. In this sense, the sexual symbolism is libertine and conservative simultaneously, a common theme in Claremont's work.

There are other noteworthy titles to discuss in Claremont's early portfolio (*Daredevil, Star Lord, Marvel Team-Up, Dr. Strange, John Carter*), but it is fair to say that the author's best and most influential work is, of course, *X-Men*, the subject of the chapter that follows.

CHAPTER TWO

Nobody Cared What We Were Doing

The Cockrum and Byrne Years

> From the moment I first saw Neal Adams' art and read Roy Thomas' scripts, I was hooked. These characters . . . spoke to me in ways that were fundamentally different from the rest of the Marvel pantheon. Perhaps that was because I'm an immigrant who spent my formative years feeling like the proverbial stranger in a strange land. Like the X-Men, I wanted to fit in. Like them, as a kid, I found that a sometimes daunting challenge.
>
> —Chris Claremont ("No Straw Dogs Here" 8)

Chris Claremont's career as a writer ultimately took off when, at the tender age of twenty-five, he was given the opportunity to write *X-Men*, a series that, despite being launched by Stan Lee and Jack Kirby in the 1960s, had failed to find a noteworthy audience and had been on hiatus for several years. In 1975, however, Roy Thomas, an editor at Marvel (and mentor to Claremont), had an idea for how to bring the X-Men back into print: "Al Landau, who was running a company that sold our pages abroad to different countries, said, 'If we had a group that had different members from different countries that we wanted to sell comics in . . .' And then I used that excuse because I wanted to bring back the X Men" (qtd. in Barnhardt n.p.). Len Wein (along with Dave Cockrum) took this idea and created *Giant-Size X-Men* as a soft relaunch of the X-Men franchise. Wein only wrote the one new X-Men issue, however, as his position was altered and he couldn't maintain the necessary schedule, so he gave the assignment to the young Claremont. "It was a very low-profile assignment since it was only a bimonthly title. No one had any great expectations for the book but the new X-Men were great characters. So, God smiled, and Len tossed it into my lap. It was like a dream come true" (Claremont qtd. in DeFalco 63).

Though credited as cowriter for *X-Men* #94–96, the stories had largely been written in advance by other writers, and so issue 97, the first whose authorship is credited to Claremont alone, is the point that Claremont identifies as where his work really began:

> I was just trying to get on my feet. The pieces were falling in place in my head, but 98 was where everything hit the fan. Dave [Cockrum] and I knew what we wanted to do and where we wanted to go from the get-go. You have to understand also that the first two issues were completing what would have been *Giant-Size X-Men* #2. The third issue was a fill-in. The fourth was taking a breath, and the next thing was learning who the characters are and figuring out where they are and what we want to do with them. By the time we got to 98 and the Sentinels were making their reentrance, we felt pressure to do a big thing for issue 100. (personal interview 2)

The team of Claremont and Cockrum landed on a definitive issue 100 in which the new X-Men team, created by the cabal of Marvel editors discussed above, do battle with robotic versions of the original X-Men, an effective symbol of the passing of the torch. With the past defeated, the new X-Men find themselves returning to planet earth in a damaged space shuttle and only Jean Grey (a holdover from the original X-Men team) can save them, but she must sacrifice herself in the process ("Greater Love Hath No X-Man . . ."). This cliffhanger carries the reader over to issue 101, where Jean's transformation to a new superhero (the celestial goddess Phoenix) sets the stage for an early example of Claremont's long-form storytelling cultivation.

From there, Claremont builds, preserves, and extends the uncertainty and mystery that surrounds Jean Grey's transformation to the superpowered cosmic goddess Phoenix, in order to throw the reader off-balance and thus add enigmatic mystery to his cosmic force. In the opening narration of UXM #101, Claremont writes, "Welcome to the last moments of a young woman's life" ("Like a Phoenix, From the Ashes"), thus stamping the extent of Jean's transformation with a compelling (and contradictory) authorial agency before Phoenix is even revealed. When she is revealed, it's with a legendary assertion of identity: "No longer am I the woman you knew. I am fire! I am life incarnate! Now and forever I am Phoenix!" (figure 2). But before taking any follow-up questions, she, of course, faints.[1]

While still in the hospital, Jean's best friend, Misty Knight (carried over from *Iron Fist* in a delightful early example of Claremont's comingling of characters from his various titles), pries into what's bothering her and Jean ominously responds, "So tell me, Misty Knight, how would you feel if you'd . . . died. Then brought yourself back to life" ("Who Will Stop the Juggernaut?" 16)? The scene ends without hearing Misty's response. Jean would not even redon her Phoenix costume until UXM #105, four months after it first appeared. This leads ultimately to the M'Kraan crystal story (UXM #107–8), which finally gives the reader a sense of who the Phoenix is and how she might fit on an X-team. The doubts would, however, continue with Cyclops's growing sense of discomfort over what Jean is and what his feelings for her are. This gets exacerbated further when Jean is separated from the rest of the team, only reuniting one arc prior to the start of the famous "Dark Phoenix Saga" storyline.

All of this is occurring at a time when the X-franchise very much does not have firm footing yet in terms of sales, so withholding this kind of dramatic reveal and lingering in these long-continuity storytelling structures is risky for a book that remains on the brink of cancellation. Clearly the reward outweighed the risk, however, with this X-mystery building toward the climactic moment in

Figure 2. Jean Grey is transformed in "Like a Phoenix, From the Ashes" (*Uncanny X-Men*, vol. 1, no. 101). Dave Cockrum, penciller.

X-Men history that is "The Dark Phoenix Saga" storyline. My point is simply that the buildup was quite bold and dramatic in ensuring the success of the series. Claremont hit the ground running with *X-Men*, and a lot of the things that make him an important comics auteur (his characters, his commitment to representation, his long, continuous story arcs) were firing on all cylinders from the very start of his run, as we see in this Phoenix-focused story arc.

While it may be impressive that Claremont would take such risks as an author at such a young age and in such a volatile medium/title, we could argue that this risk-taking was specifically empowered by lower-than-usual stakes on the title. Through this, Claremont and Cockrum were given free rein to experiment, thus empowering the cultivation of new methods of comics storytelling. In an interview, Claremont notes, "I could evolve the X-Men because nobody gave a fuck" (personal interview 1). Furthermore, low sales had the effect of siloing a series from the broader business model. As Claremont notes, "My *X-Men* run got a chance to define itself in its own unique manner without having to worry about toys, videos—the exploitative aspects" (personal interview 1). Claremont's talent is his own, but his circumstances were ideal in empowering him to make use of it successfully. Not every writer gets that opportunity.

At the same time, we should note that while the underdog mentality certainly applied to Claremont at the time, Dave Cockrum had already established himself as an elite illustrator and character designer, so much so that it's safe to say that Cockrum's art was the real drawing point for the early issues of the Claremont run on *X-Men*, thus providing Claremont with a platform through which to establish his own following. Eisner Award–winning editor and writer Tom Spurgeon describes Cockrum's contribution as follows:

> It's easy to underestimate Cockrum's penciled art in the book itself. Cockrum's penciled interiors on those first few issues of the "new" *X-Men* were dark and appealingly dramatic; in keeping with the book's more serious themes, the evocation of superpowers in the

stories was often depicted as dirty and painful, and his characters were for the most part weathered adults instead of smooth-faced children—in a time near the end of the Cold War when that distinction mattered. Cockrum gave those first few issues of *X-Men* a sumptuous, late-'70s cinema style that separated the book from the rest of Marvel's line, and superhero comics in general. Reading those *X-Men* comics felt like sneaking into a movie starring Sean Connery or Sigourney Weaver, something for adults because it featured people that looked like adults. *Uncanny X-Men* really felt new and different, almost right away, and Cockrum's art was a tremendous part of that. (Spurgeon n.p.)

Claremont himself notes, "I was the luckiest of young writers: in Dave Cockrum the book had not simply a superb visual storyteller but one of the benchmark character designers in comics history" ("No Straw Dogs Here" 8).

By 1977, however, Dave Cockrum was struggling to balance a new promotion at Marvel, his home life, and his artist's obligations to Uncanny X-Men, the title that he had helped to reinvigorate with the aid of first Len Wein and then Chris Claremont. John Byrne was a prolific young talent in the Marvel bullpen at the time. He had already worked successfully with Claremont on a number of other titles, but, with their pairing on *X-Men*, we got what has gone down in history as one of the most famous collaborations in comics. Byrne's first issue on the run was titled "Armageddon Now," and true to that title it features an enormous roster of characters, including iconic Marvel superhero guest stars such as the Avengers and the Fantastic Four; a dizzying amount of outer space action scenes; and a completely surreal culminating sequence in which a celestial being stitches together the fabric of the universe itself. In short, the degree of difficulty for any illustrator would be beyond all reasonable expectation, and Byrne delivers a beautifully penciled issue.

Byrne's intricately detailed penciling, with soft curves, clear lines, and a delicate expertise with perspective, set a new standard for comics illustration. In a series that had previously boasted penciling runs by Jack Kirby, Neal Adams, and Cockrum, Byrne's artwork still stood out. For legendary comics scholar Richard Reynolds, it was John Byrne's approach to subjective perspective in his artwork that led to the immersive character identification of *UXM*: "Byrne employed a style of sequential art that was 'cinematic' in the sense that it constantly interpreted each panel and each segment of the narrative from an implied and subjective point of view. The reader was drawn in, invited to take sides in the characters' conflicts" (*Super Heroes* 86). Simply put, Byrne adopted the cinematic approach of locating the angle of perception in such a way as to locate the reader within the scene according to the demands of the story as it was unfolding—using his camera, so to speak, to define the relationship of the reader to the action depicted. If the scene requires Wolverine to be intimidating, for example, have him stare right at you with his claws out. If it requires you to be in awe of the heroes, have the reader looking up at them as if they are (literally and figuratively) above you. The process is fluid and can vary from panel to panel. As Reynolds notes, "Each character's point of view can be played up as required. Byrne's skill with 'camera angles' involves and includes the reader in the construction of the narrative" (*Super Heroes* 86). The effect of this approach is complex—it creates immersion, obviously, by locating the reader in every scene, but that immersion has important cascading effects on things like suspension of disbelief, emotional impact, narrative tension, and character empathy. This is all to say that Byrne's work (greatly enhanced by the inks of Terry Austin) is more than just "illustrative," that a lot of the depth and impact of the broader narrative components is coming directly from the artwork (including inks and colors), taking Claremont's scripts to entirely new levels of engagement and empowering Claremont to pursue greater nuance in his own storytelling.

Indeed, at this point in Claremont's carer his entire creative team was composed of individuals who, though mostly just starting out in their careers, would all go on to become esteemed figures in their

Figure 3. "Armageddon Now" (*Uncanny X-Men*, vol. 1, no. 108). Art by John Byrne and Terry Austin. John Byrne, penciller.

respective fields. Editor Roger Stern describes working with the full team as "Fun. Big fun. Wondrous fun. Chris, by that point, was already a very good wordsmith, and he brought a lot of passion to his work. Ditto for John on the pencils. They could butt heads as to story direction, but there was a great synergy between the two of them" ("Interview with Roger Stern" n.p.). When asked what made this particular run so memorable, Stern replies, "They were a bunch of young guys getting a chance to prove themselves with a book that had at best been a minor seller. And they produced a consistently good comic that got better every issue. . . . It was 'the' comic of the hour" ("Interview with Roger Stern" n.p.). If there's a lesson here on the importance of comics writers surrounding themselves with elite talent, Claremont learned it. As his later editor in chief Jim Shooter noted in an interview about Claremont, the author's commitment to his team was quite rare and included paying collaborators like letterer Tom Orzechowski and colorist Glynnis Oliver out of pocket in order to retain their services "because he was married to that book." Shooter also notes, "He was the only guy that did that" ("Jim Shooter Biographical Interview" n.p.)

By *UXM* #114, Byrne began being credited as coplotter. Together, the duo walked the X-Men through paradigm-altering, iconic stories such as "The Dark Phoenix Saga" and "Days of Future Past," launching properties such as the Hellfire Club, Alpha Flight, the Shadow King, Proteus, Rachel Summers, and, of course, Kitty Pryde. With each issue of the collaboration, the popularity of the book increased—a trend of prosperity and critical praise[2] that would continue right through the end of Byrne's tenure on the series, though the exact nature of that ending has been a bit elusive and somewhat contested, with Byrne arguing that he was upset because he did not receive enough credit for his storytelling contributions to the series. "I realized that the Chris version of the characters was what was seeing print. The way Chris wrote it was what was seeing print, regardless of what I thought it was in my head while I was drawing the pages" (qtd. in DeFalco 114). In the wake of the split, Claremont was free to plot X-Men his way again and Byrne was free to distinguish himself on other famous comics projects, completing iconic runs on *Fantastic Four*, *Man of Steel*, and *She-Hulk*.

The success of the Claremont/Byrne run (and before it the Claremont/Cockrum run) was, as indicated previously in this volume, as much a question of character as anything—a clear feedback loop in which the cultivation of iconic comics characters struck a chord with a generation of comics readers. As noted, Claremont inherited most of his X-Men from previous writers. The majority of these characters was relatively fresh, having appeared in less than five issues of comics previously, and often with very little character development. As Claremont says himself in and interview, "With X-Men, I had the good fortune of coming in right at the start. With the characters that Len and Dave created, all we knew was a paragraph describing them. It was all virgin territory" (personal interview 2). What he did with that territory within the context of this superhero soap opera that he articulated with the help of legendary comics creators is, arguably, his greatest accomplishment as a writer and deserves a bit of unpacking in terms of who these characters became and how the author cultivated them.

Three of the characters that Claremont inherited on X-Men were written out of the series within the first few years. Sunfire quit almost immediately, though Claremont would integrate him in a later storyline set in Sunfire's native Japan. Banshee stuck with the team until just before "The Dark Phoenix Saga" began but Claremont did little with the character other than establish a relationship with Moira MacTaggert, an important side character in the series. Banshee too would return in a later arc as a key player in the rebirth era of *X-Men*, discussed in a later chapter. Perhaps the most controversial departure, however, was Thunderbird, an Apache character at a time when Indigenous superheroes were quite rare in Marvel Comics.

Claremont has taken heat for the death of Thunderbird, which is a little unfair as he did not actually plot that departure and himself opposed it: "I was sad that we killed off Thunderbird because having an Indigenous character on the team would have made it more interesting" (personal interview 2). Nonetheless, the death of Thunderbird was executed in the pages of *X-Men* #94–95 at the behest of departing editor Len Wein. The reaction was mixed, as scholar Jeremy Carnes notes, "As early as *The X-Men* #97, Marvel printed a letter from Tom Runningmouth, a self-identified American Indian, who writes, 'I was proud to see one of my people, an American Indian—America's First citizens—become a member but to my dissatisfaction in *X-Men* #94, you started to oppress him. But the clincher was in *X-Men* #95. You killed him. Why was he chosen? Why Thunderbird?'" (58). Carnes also quotes the response by Len Wein and Dave Cockrum, who suggest that John Proudstar "had nowhere to go. All he was, all he really ever could be, was a wisecracking, insolent, younger, not-as-interesting copy of Hawkeye" (58). Carnes takes issue with this explanation, however, calling it "mired in white settler colonial discourse" and suggesting that "Thunderbird had to die because Wein and Cockrum could not envision a Native character that existed in the present" (58–59). Claremont would later be able to pull off such a feat of imagination (to some degree) with his later creation of key Indigenous characters such as Forge, Moonstar, Silver Fox, Shaman, and James (John's brother).

In the meantime, Claremont set to work developing the remaining X-Men as complex characters to differing levels of success. The character of Storm (Ororo Munroe)—arguably the centerpiece of his X-Men run—can very much be seen as a representational milestone. Storm was initially created through a recycling of comics characters previously designed by Dave Cockrum for an unused pitch called "The Outsiders," then amalgamated together for X-Men with the help of Len Wein and Roy Thomas at Marvel ("Dave Cockrum's Outsiders" n.p.). Under Claremont, Storm would become both Marvel's first female superhero team leader and also their first Black team leader. In her seminal volume *Superwomen*, Carolyn Cocca refers to Storm, more generally, as comics' "first major black superheroine" (125).

The reasons for this generalized major-ness are complicated, but scholar Anita McDaniels offers a concise perspective in stating, "Storm is an important black female character in the Marvel Universe because she has been drawn and written to be important. Few black or female characters (not to mention black *and* female characters) have achieved her status as a superhero" (121–22). Deborah Whaley accounts for Storm's overall impact in writing that Storm's character arc under Claremont "represents a visionary social subject that propels social change" (107). However we frame it, the consistent factor in Storm's importance is depth. So how did Claremont achieve that with/for her?

Let's start with relatable symbolism and subsequent vulnerability. Storm's claustrophobia is one of the earliest elements introduced of her character, serving a litany of purposes and offering a rare sympathetic portrayal of an anxiety disorder in superhero comics. The disorder humanizes Storm by connecting to her traumatic past, asserting not just that she's vulnerable (and thus relatable) but also that she has a history, a lineage, and a tragedy behind her, all of which help to define and humanize the character. At the same time, from an action perspective, Claremont uses claustrophobia as Storm's kryptonite, providing the writer with a compelling and human way to sideline his most overpowered character in order to add tension and stakes to action scenes. Symbolically, Storm's claustrophobia contributes to her metaphorical engagement with the conflict between nature and civilization. We see this through the ways that story (and especially visuals) frequently emphasize her need to fly high above the enclosed urban environments she's been made to inhabit. There are some sexist tropes that the claustrophobia runs the risk of serving—most notably the concept of feminine hysteria—but given Storm's power, agency, and centrality in X-Men comics, her condition might instead become a more nuanced consideration of how even the best superheroes can struggle.

Claremont also writes contrast into Storm's character by exploring the juxtaposition between her sense of willful passion and her sense of interiority and self-isolation. Perhaps even more than iconic loner Wolverine, Ororo often needs to withdraw and be alone. We first see it in the aftermath of the team's battle with Garokk from X-Men #116 ("To Save the Savage Land"). Storm desperately tries to save the villain from death, but she is overcome by her own claustrophobia and she fails. She grieves alone, and Wolverine can see clearly that she needs her space to do so. We also see it when she revisits her childhood home in Harlem. Wolverine demands to chaperone her, but she simply informs him, "What I do today, I must do alone" (12). Her famous connection to nature (a connection with compelling connections to the discourse of ecofeminism) is important here as well. Storm likes to be alone, to fly high above the maddening crowd with just nature surrounding her. It's how she decompresses and is clearly a solitary ritual. Importantly, Storm's isolation isn't born of necessity—she is surrounded by people who love her, people she loves back, but she still requires space. The isolationism isn't presented as a character flaw, either. It's simply her process, in sharp contrast to the distinctive processes of other X-Men.

Despite Storm's centrality in the series, the breakout character of the early years of Claremont's *X-Men* is, clearly, Wolverine (Logan). Initially viewed as somewhat disposable by both Claremont and Marvel editorial, Wolverine (particularly under the guidance of John Byrne) blossomed into a dynamic and compelling character. Claremont's most notable work with the property would come after Byrne's departure, however—transitioning Logan from a killing machine into a noble hero. As Grant Morrison notes, "The same delicate touch transformed the Wolverine character from a one-note 'feisty scrapper' to a layered portrayal of a man torn between nobility and savagery. Claremont gave a soul to his modern samurai, and Wolverine became a breakout hit character" (176).

In their early character cultivation, we can see Claremont and Byrne establishing Wolverine as an isolationist loner with a sense of values that are notably self-defined. Travis Smith argues, "Wolverine's sense of honor is personal. He does not defer to the standards of the communities he serves; he serves them in accordance with his own code. Admittedly, this makes it hard to distinguish his code from a subjective set of personal values" (23). This may put Wolverine into the same category as someone like *Watchmen*'s Rorschach, Alan Moore's commentary on the problematic veneration of subjective morality in superhero comics. Smith further notes, "Wolverine maintains his code of honor despite the fact that within his social context he enjoys neither legal permission nor moral approval to execute his self-imposed obligations in the frightful fashion he does" (23). Smith also suggests that Wolverine's self-defined values can be read in a heroic way (if read generously) as a commentary on the cost of civilized living at the expense of self-definition itself—in a manner that is almost analogous to Freud's discussions on the necessity of repression. "Maybe his self-conception is misguided or ridiculous, even worthy of reproach. Read generously, he reminds us that something important has been given up in order for us to realize the way of life we now enjoy" (23). In all of this, then, Wolverine can be seen to speak to something fundamental in human nature with direct relevance to the found family metaphor that Claremont articulates in *X-Men*.

Outside of his values, it is worth noting that Claremont and Byrne do inscribe in Logan a key point of vulnerability that speaks to the inherent conflict between the inward-looking and outward-facing aspects of his character. Logan is seen to be weak to chaos—to being thrown off-balance. We first see this in a trap set by Arcade in *Uncanny X-Men* #123 ("Listen—Stop Me If You've Heard It—But This One Will Kill You!")—a funhouse of mirrors that confronts Wolverine with multiple distorted versions of himself followed by robot embodiments that attack and disorient him to a pointed effect on his senses. The theme then takes further shape in Logan's encounter with Proteus in *Uncanny X-Men* #128, where the villain assails Wolverine with wild distortions of reality that leave Logan deeply shaken, even prompting a PTSD-like distress in the usually confident and unflappable X-Man ("The

Action of the Tiger"). The theme resurfaces again, however, in *Uncanny X-Men* #137 when Logan wanders into Uatu's home and finds himself exposed (or overexposed) to the complexity of the multiverse and the grandiose timescale by which Uatu lives and operates ("The Fate of the Phoenix!"). It recurs again in Dr. Doom's castle as a technique by which Doom can confuse and control Wolverine. This last encounter spurs a direct reflection for Logan on his broader battle with his primitive urges, even triggering a flashback that helps Wolverine find the will to escape Doom's trap ("Rogue Storm!" 16). This weakness is explored extensively throughout Claremont's entire run and is a very interesting choice for the character, symbolically conveying the constant struggle of a man who is striving to hold himself together and grounded, one who fears losing himself to the berserker rages that likewise rob him of all rationality. Thus, Claremont's choice of practical weakness for Logan parallels the character's larger existential vulnerability to pointed effect, helping to make Wolverine, like Storm, deeply relatable as a result of competing dualities and subsequent vulnerability.

For the character of Nightcrawler (Kurt Wagner), Claremont and Cockrum saw an opportunity to subvert the Frankenstein/Ben Grimm archetype of tortured monstrosity by instead building the character out of self-acceptance. This allows Kurt to speak to different symbologies: "And once you cross that line and say, 'It's not my problem. It's how you choose to look at me, not how I am. This is who I am. Accept it or not, but it's not my fault.' That gives you, as a writer, a tremendous amount of freedom to comment on how people perceive other people" (personal interview 1). This reading is quite common with how many read Nightcrawler and indeed why many people specifically love and identify with the character, such as scholar Anna Peppard, who notes that "Nightcrawler wears his weirdness with pride, laughs in the face of danger, and when he's not locking swords with undead pirates, space pirates, or holographic pirates, he combats hate with compassion (this sometimes involves jump-kicking bigots in the face, but I'll allow it)" (n.p.).

As *UXM* grew ever darker and deeper, Kurt Wagner stood out as a rare joyous character, someone who relished the role of showman, and though Claremont, at times, punished him for this inclination, he also found spaces to let Kurt thrive. Kurt's theatrical nature was quickly identified (and very nearly stamped out) by his field leader, Cyclops, in *UXM* #99: "You're not in the circus anymore, mister. That kind of flamboyance can cost us if you're not careful." Kurt's response, however, is an assertion of his identity: "I have been a showman all my life, Cyclops. . . . It is in my blood and I'm not about to change for you—or anyone!" ("Deathstar, Rising!"). This assertion of identity would prove to be prophetic for Claremont's treatment of the character as an outsider who was radically committed to his own self-acceptance.

Perhaps relatedly, we should note that, though it never made it to print, Nightcrawler was nearly the vehicle through which Claremont might have made his most radical representation of queer families in the 1970s/1980s. In his 2011 article "The Feminine Mystique: Feminism, Sexuality, Motherhood," scholar Ross Murray laments the opportunity to subvert patriarchal values that was lost when Claremont was not allowed by Marvel to make the female-presenting shapeshifter character Mystique[3] Nightcrawler's father:

> Mystique and Destiny raising a birthed child together as lesbians (as opposed to the fostering of Rogue) is a lapse from the common family unit. Indeed the idea of self-sufficient females doing the job by themselves poses an imminent threat to patriarchal culture not minimally by bypassing the male as producer of the heroic seed. Mystique and Destiny would have instigated a parthenogenetic matriarchy representing a major challenge to superhero patriarchy. These women then specifically occupy Barbara Creed's function of the monstrous which is to "bring about an encounter between the symbolic order and that which threatens its stability" (1993, p. 11). Creepy, disturbing, eerie, unsettling, uncanny—a woman occupying the male's procreative role is positively monstrous. Mystique threatens the male progenitor's role with dissolution. (11)

This never came to pass, however, for, as Claremont recounts, "Everyone thought it was a little too creepy for words" (personal interview 2).

Where Nightcrawler offered avenues to explore the concepts of self and social acceptance, his teammate Colossus (Piotr Rasputin) offered a rare opportunity to humanize the enemy of an American audience's geopolitical opponent of the time. When Colossus debuted in 1975, America was embroiled in the Cold War with the USSR, a war that was often fought through media propaganda. Though Piotr was built around familiar US symbols of Soviet caricature, Claremont developed him away from type. Steel and agriculture were dominant symbols of the USSR at the time (seen on their flag), so a farm boy who turns to living steel is right in-line with type from the get-go. His costume also features the colors of the Soviet flag, and he espouses communist philosophy. In "Asymmetric Warfare: The Vision of the Enemy in American and Soviet Cold War Cinemas," Andrey Shcherbenok establishes US mass culture's tendency to portray Soviet persons in media as homogenized, generic enemies, overdetermined by their hate of America: "American tradition was never overly dependent on the ideological content of the conflict and could largely continue into the present by replacing Communists with Arab terrorists, international mafia, transnational syndicates and other enemies of the free world" (12–13). Thus, an enemy of America was simply an enemy of America with no more development or cultivation beyond that fundamental identity marker. Where Claremont complicates Piotr's conformity to type is simply in the cultivation of his individual identity. By giving Piotr agency, humanity, motivations, and flaws, Piotr achieved escape velocity from USSR stereotypes. Claremont notably called attention to this in *Uncanny X-Men* #124, where Piotr does indeed allow himself to think in a generic and nationalistic self/other binary before breaking his conditioning in order to make choices based on individualistic values of friendship and family ("He Only Laughs When I Hurt!"). Post–Cold War, today's readers might not really even see the full significance of a sympathetic and heroic portrayal of a Soviet citizen, but during the Cold War, Piotr Rasputin's humanity was itself an important representational milestone.

Speaking to more specific aspects of Piotr's character, Claremont's Colossus is repeatedly presented as someone who struggles with big emotions to match his big physique but who also routinely stifles and represses said emotions beneath a veneer of stoicism. Where many other characters demonstrate a capacity to explore their emotions within the found family dynamic of the X-Men team (or even just subgroups within the team, such as Storm and Logan's mutual respect), Piotr prefers to be alone and is largely incapable of such expression. Considering the length of his tenure on the team, Piotr has shockingly few speech or thought bubbles, but when we do get his internal monologue, Claremont presents him as a thoughtful young man, intensely focused on his own perceived inadequacies. In one instance Wolverine (always presented by Claremont as an astute and intuitive reader of people) quickly identifies that Piotr thrives on emotion and uses the young man's concern for his friends to motivate him, even while Cyclops (approaching things tactically) fails to get the results sought ("Cry for the Children!"). We also see Piotr fly into full-on berserker rages (not unlike Logan's) when he feels that his friends have been hurt or threatened somehow. All of this speaks again to the depth of Claremont's characters but also, as mentioned, to the consistency with which he writes their voices as distinct individuals. Even Piotr, arguably Claremont's least-developed X-Man, has a complex psychology to him.

Of all the characters that Claremont cultivated in this era, with the help of his A-team of collaborators, the most notable might be the first X-Man that he created from scratch: Kitty Pryde, a character who, in the eyes of many scholars on the subject of X-Men, played an enormous role in changing the superhero comics landscape.

In her essay "From Kitty to Cat: Kitty Pryde and the Phases of Feminism," Margaret Galvan argues that Kitty Pryde can be seen to represent transgressive gender politics, that Kitty's phasing challenges "notions of stability at their most basic, physical level. How she employs these transgressive powers in concert with a plucky persona make Pryde an often-overlooked powerhouse and a figure of the multivalent feminism that thrived in the 1980s" (47–48). Kitty is a teenage mutant Jewish girl genius, and all of these aspects define her, even (if not especially) when they create friction: "All of these simultaneously ever-present identities embody the concerns of 1980s feminism by putting pressure on monolithic ideas of identity" (50). As Galvan notes, this transgressive potential manifests multiple times throughout the run, with Kitty frequently challenging other characters for thinking within one-dimensional paradigms. Thus, she vocalizes the same transgressive symbols that she embodies.

The symbolic potential of the character only increased as Claremont pushed Kitty from a minor character to a central viewpoint character within the series—a move that ultimately impacted the series, comics as a whole, and potentially even Western media in powerful ways. The Claremont run begins with Cyclops as the main viewpoint character (a structure inherited from all the X-Men comics that came before Claremont). Kitty joins the team right at his departure and soon enough takes over as the main viewpoint character for the rest of her tenure. At the time of her arrival, Claremont and collaborators had already executed a turn toward more adult-oriented stories in the series. It's therefore perhaps odd to bring on a teen protagonist. Kitty's capability is immediately established, however, first with a "Days of Future Past" story arc that establishes her position of prominence in the team's future, then immediately after that in a solo story that sees her defeating a demon by herself in what would be John Byrne's last issue of the series ("Demon"). Once established, Kitty carries more and more of the viewpoint character role in the series. That role is always distributed across different characters but never equally, and Kitty quickly becomes Claremont's go-to.

This transition has a number of notable effects: First, it creates a greater sense of parity between the protagonist's age and that of the series's implied/intended audience, making immersion into the X-Men's world that much easier for younger readers. Second, instead of allowing Kitty to make the text more juvenile, Claremont persists in his depiction of horrific experiences using Kitty's sense of being overwhelmed (despite her capability) to enhance the sense of vulnerability and tension within the series overall. Third, having an emotionally vulnerable hero take center stage in a conflict between superpowered beings presents opportunities to speak to the cost of the conflict in much more human and relatable terms, leading to a more nuanced representation of emotional toll. Finally, we have to note that even though X-Men was already defying the masculinist norms of the superhero genre at the time of Kitty's arrival, having a thirteen-year-old girl serve as the protagonist of a superhero adventure comic was wholly unique. Galvan notes, "Fighting against expectations, Pryde extends the field of what powerful superheroines look and act like" (47). That she did so from a position of prominence, and that it worked so well, serves as testament to the character's legacy.

As much as character is Claremont's greatest strength as a writer, his collaboration with John Byrne also produced what is, arguably, the most iconic storyline in the history of X-Men comics: "The Dark Phoenix Saga." The influence of Dark Phoenix is everywhere. As noted by Julian Darius of Sequart, the work of comics legend Alan Moore was directly inspired by "The Dark Phoenix Saga" when creating his Marvelman (later retitled "Miracleman") series (n.p.). It's also entered the cultural lexicon with "Dark ___" referencing a version of a beloved character who turns evil through unchecked power—a famous example of this would be the "Dark Willow" storyline from *Buffy the Vampire Slayer* season 6, or even broader story arcs in comics like "Dark Avengers." This influence is well earned and, as an apex moment in Claremont's early X-Men work, "The Dark Phoenix Saga" merits a closer look in itself.

The first thing to note about "The Dark Phoenix Saga" is that boundaries are a little tricky. Claremont spends a lot of time sowing seeds of DPS, and isolating a true beginning is challenging (arguably it goes back to UXM #97) but most collected editions like to isolate the aftermath of the Proteus story arc in UXM #129 as the start of DPS. From there, the X-Men are attacked by an emerging foe on two fronts: Piotr, Ororo, Logan (and Kitty) are captured by the White Queen, while the illusionist villain Mastermind manipulates Jean's conscious and subconscious mind in order to turn her to his side. This leads, ultimately, to the reveal of the broader Hellfire Club and Jean's unwilling betrayal of the team before the Hellfire Club is defeated and the X-Men head home. What seems like a very natural resolution point is interrupted without the intervention of a direct villain. Mastermind is defeated but the damage to Jean's psyche is done and Jean's dark side breaks through, creating a new conflict even within the aftermath of the previous one. The X-Men then rise to the occasion and defeat Jean with the power of technology, love, and an epic telepathic duel that highlights the downright cosmic scope of Professor Xavier's power, not to mention his commitment, thus forming another natural endpoint. Yet again, however, Claremont hits us with consequences instead of resolution. During her initial manifestation, Dark Phoenix had attacked the alien Shi'ar and killed an entire planet. She has to answer for that, and the reader is immediately thrown into the next round of conflict—the final fight with the Shi'ar Royal Guard, which is only resolved with Jean's demise by suicide.

These conflicts are different but clearly connected, with each one leading naturally to the next rather than leading straight into the arms of an entirely new conflict. This continuity and integration (discussed previously) creates a through line that allows for greater internal cohesion. By exploring the same overarching conflict through the lens of multiple connected conflicts, DPS is able to present a more nuanced portrayal of conflict in general, one that accounts for competing interests and multifaceted consequences.

The emotional centerpiece of the storyline is, clearly, the death of Jean Grey, an original X-Man.[4] Famously, Jean Grey's death was written into *UXM* #137 at the last minute due to editorial demand, and while most fans and scholars consider it a milestone development for the franchise, the initial response of the fans was not always positive. In the letters page of *UXM* #143, you can find a famous fan expressing deep outrage with Claremont's take on X-Men and with "The Dark Phoenix Saga" in particular:

> But for the past two years (since #113) I've watched the book degenerate, watched the X-Men become a perversion of what they once were, watched you twist and mangle characters you virtually created. I first decided to stop buying during the "Hellfire Club" storyline but held on for sentimental reasons and a vague hope that things would get better. During the "Dark Phoenix" story, I again decided to quit, but upon hearing what the conclusion would be, I decided to stick around 'til Cyclops left. And now, I can no longer justify buying the X-Men, not even to keep my collection complete. Each issue hurts too much. I love the X-Men, and if you treated them as they deserve, I would still be a faithful supporter, but until matters change, you've lost yourself a reader. (qtd. in "Demon")

The letter is signed: "Kurt Busiek," a young man who would later make his fame as the author of *Astro City* and *Marvels*. As a fun aside, it was actually Busiek who came up with the idea for Jean Grey's resurrection years later.

As villains go, the Hellfire Club in "The Dark Phoenix Saga" also allows Claremont the opportunity to begin complicating the us versus them aspects of the mutants in society context of the X-Men in favor of more complex politics. Throughout the history of the franchise, mutants were presented as a powerless minority (despite superpowers), forced to either violently oppose humankind or seek allyship with humankind. They are in a weak and vulnerable position. The Hellfire Club's inner circle is composed almost entirely of mutants, however, operating as "an exclusive, ultrasecret cabal dedicated to the acquisition of power for its members" (Papers) even to the point of lobbying the US government to reopen the Sentinels program (those mutant-hunting robots again). The idea of mutants in a position of ultimate power behind the scenes is compelling, as is their lack of loyalty to the mutant cause—preferring instead the blanket pursuit of power even to the point of the destruction of their fellow mutants. In this variation from the established binary mutant/human struggle, we can then read the idea of cultural divide as a distraction from the genuine power struggles of the world since the Hellfire Club simply leverage and commodify majority/minority conflict for their own financial interest. They don't really care about mutants or humans except that other people do, and they can use that to their advantage in order to consolidate wealth and power. This development would add some sophistication to *UXM* in later years through the uneasy alliances that key X-Men personnel have to make with the Hellfire Club in order to escape, to some degree, the simpler game that they (and the reader) had been stuck in before.

We must also note, however, the aesthetic of the Hellfire Club and its capacity to draw Claremont's sexual subtext toward the surface. This aesthetic has been described as "flagrant fetish attire" by Jason Powell (46), but there's a level of complexity and subtlety to the representation that has captivated other scholars in a different way. In an essay titled "Emma Frost, the White Queen: Superpowers as the Performance of Gender," scholar Richard Reynolds explores the ways that Frost complicates her hypersexual appearance through layers of irony and empowerment. For Reynolds, Frost is a "sexual terrorist" who surfaces "the fetish subtext long encoded in superheroine (and villainess) costumes" in order to "subvert the established power structures of the genre while simultaneously being the object of the male gaze. . . . Frost's self-empowering manipulation of the male gaze—and herself as the object of the gaze—not only subverts deeply inscribed conventions of the superhero genre, but also deregulates binary distinctions between object and subject" ("Emma Frost" 122). As these accounts suggest, the sexuality of the Hellfire Club can be read as either flagrant or subversive, or possibly both simultaneously, and that's actually a pretty good account of Claremont's portrayal of sexuality in general.

The coda for "The Dark Phoenix Saga" is delivered in UXM #138 and might serve, arguably, as a worthy coda both for the Byrne collaboration (he would leave over creative differences five issues later) and for this era of X-Men in general. The framing of the issue is very similar to issue #2 of Alan Moore and Dave Gibbons's Watchmen, which would come out six years later. Both juxtapose scenes of a funeral with snapshots of the past in order to create a sense of grim destiny for the story being told (knowing where it's headed). Jean's funeral scene contains no dialogue in order to emphasize the silence of the moment (simulating grief) right up until the very end, when Cyclops announces his departure, thus breaking the silence with something of a crescendo. Claremont's scripting is some of his best—the content is mostly irrelevant (just a recap of old issues), but the tone is heartbreaking as we hear Scott Summers describe the adventures of his life through a newly developed sense of bitterness and futility. It's through this voice that Scott comes to question the very meaning of his existence as the X-Man Cyclops. "This . . . is pain beyond pain. I never knew a body could hurt so much and still . . . function. I'm not sure I want to call this 'living'" ("Elegy" n.p.). Scott's tone in the issue is also what makes his decision to leave make sense in some way. The reader is made to inhabit the character's anguished perspective—drowning in his same grief—and thus needing the same relief that Scott does. The issue, all about the concept of endings, itself ends (somewhat paradoxically) with a beginning: a brief teaser showing nothing more than the arrival of Kitty Pryde and a caption that warns the reader of the new era to come: "Her name, as you may have guessed, is Kitty Pryde. She's about to become the newest—and youngest—pupil in Charles Xavier's school. The X-Men will never be the same again!" ("Elegy" n.p.). And, of course, the changes that this arrival brought to the series are the subject of our next chapter.

CHAPTER THREE

The Long Game

The Smith and Romita Era

> But these heroes' lives? It's reality. Not living in their own secure bubble, but living in a space and time that readers can recognize as their own, and building situations that we can relate to as people.
> —Chris Claremont ("I'm Chris Claremont ")

With Byrne's departure from the series, Claremont was empowered to take the existing momentum of the franchise and channel it toward his personal vision for the X-Men. Though sometimes overshadowed by the bombast of the Cockrum or Byrne eras, it's during this time period that Claremont most readily demonstrates his growing commitment to long-form continuity, to shifting the status quo of comics, and, most especially, to building what would go on to become what Jay Edidin and Miles Stokes have coined "comics greatest superhero soap opera."

One of the more important (and influential) shifts in direction during this era is the transition from bronze age conceptions of good versus evil to a more modern sensibility (a process arguably begun with the Hellfire Club, as discussed in the previous chapter). We see this transition quite clearly in the 1982 X-Men graphic novel, *God Loves, Man Kills*. Scholar Carlos Caldas notes that the story in *God Loves, Man Kills* executes a rare shift from typical superhero symbolism by using supernatural love, rather than supernatural powers to save the day (86): The X-Men confront villain William Stryker with words, in the end, not fists. This broad departure from moral absolutism and violent justice is pivotal for the franchise and might even help to define mainstream comics' broader transition from the bronze to modern age, a transition that Claremont's X-Men comics were an important part of according to scholars such as Richard Reynolds (*Superheroes*) and Roger Sabin. As the series moves forward in the wake of *God Loves, Man Kills*, binary depictions of good and evil continue to vanish behind flawed heroes making mistakes and righteous villains making a frightening amount of sense. This is a sharp contrast to the early years of the run, and *GLMK* might indeed be the tipping point.

Shortly after its publication, the mainline *Uncanny X-Men* series introduced another elite artist (following a return run from Dave Cockrum) who would empower Claremont's commitment to character-based melodrama even further. In 1983, Paul Smith was invited to become the full-time X-Men illustrator after drawing the team in an issue of *Marvel Fanfare*. He would last only ten issues before leaving, but he left an indelible mark on both the artwork and the creative direction of the franchise.

Smith was a Steve Ditko devotee; his dream was to draw Spider-Man or Conan, and he saw his time on *UXM* as a stepping stone toward those other titles. Influenced by Smith's fantastic grasp of gesture, posture, and expression, Claremont's *X-Men* turned more toward the soap opera during this era by featuring key romantic developments for Wolverine, Cyclops, Kitty/Colossus, and Nightcrawler. In an interview at the time of first taking the assignment, Smith promised, "People are built differently. But that's what I hope to deal with: different body structures. People will move differently, people will be built differently, people will react differently" (qtd. in Thompson n.p.). This differentiation of bodies, movements, and reactions was pivotal in individualizing (and thus humanizing) Claremont's characters to a further degree and thus greatly enhancing Claremont's ongoing commitment to character nuance.

This aesthetic transition (in tandem with Claremont's narrative transition toward moral complexity) is further enhanced by Bob

Figure 4. "Professor Xavier Is a Jerk!" (*Uncanny X-Men*, vol. 1, no. 168). Art by Paul Smith and Bob Wiacek. Paul Smith, penciller.

Wiacek, who inked issues #159–76 with a distinctive style that did little to imitate his predecessors and everything to push toward the future. Wiacek's inks represented a major stylistic departure for the series. Though capable of drawing out the same thick, high-contrast shadows as Terry Austin, Wiacek's preference was to create more negative space within the panels in contrast to Austin's detailed shading and hatching. This stylistic deviation (which was also less labor-intensive) drew out the precision of Paul Smith's figure drawings in particular, creating an open visual theme that was inviting and soft, perfectly suited, once again, to the series's transition toward more character-based melodrama.

Perhaps surprisingly at the time (given concerns over Byrne's departure), readership increased during Smith's run, and the series locked into a more fluid, character-driven format that would stay with the book long after Smith left. The thing that still astonishes most about Smith's time is just the sheer volume of iconic images and panel layouts that he produced in a short span of issues. Something about his artwork simply sticks with the fandom.

Empowered by this new aesthetic, Claremont's soap opera structure can be seen quite clearly by the time the series reaches issues #168–71—an arc that marks a key transition point from space opera (Cockrum's specialty and preference) to soap opera. Themes of relationship politics work their way into both the A-story and the various B-stories explored throughout this span of issues, all of which leads us to the next arc, which is (appropriately) the wedding of Logan and Mariko. In the buildup to that event, we see Cyclops seeking out and achieving resolution in his post-Jean rebound relationship with Lee Forester. From there, Cyclops meets a new paramour, Madelyne Pryor, and pursues a relationship with her based in honesty and transparency about both his past relationship with Jean and his mutant powers. We also get a brief glimpse of Nightcrawler's casual, sex-positive relationship with the stewardess/sorceress Amanda Sefton; several scenes chronicling Lilandra's emotional support of Xavier through his recovery from his physical injuries; and Callisto's abduction of Angel juxtaposed with Caliban's abduction of Kitty. We also get a rare early glimpse of the subtextually queer couple Mystique and Destiny sharing domestic space and supporting each other emotionally. The series would shift directions again after Smith's departure but never wholly abandon the soap opera component or fail to trade on the gains of character development produced in this era.

The next penciller to step in (midway through issue #175 in fact) was John Romita Jr., and he too left his mark on Claremont's storytelling, with Sean Howe noting, "Once John Romita Jr. replaced Smith, though, the darker elements of *X-Men* gradually came to the fore" (286). Unlike Smith, JRJR (as he's sometimes called) had a long tenure on the series, penciling more issues of Claremont's *UXM* than any other illustrator with the exception of John Byrne (who beat him by just three issues). In spite of this, and in spite of Romita's later fame, his contribution to *UXM* has often been critically underserved. Romita's low-detail, rough-edged figure drawing was a jarring contrast from previous X-Men illustrators, which may have alienated fans, but this gritty style suited dark storylines such as "The Mutant Massacre" quite effectively, and his infusion of punk elements from the emerging alternative comics scene (paired with the house style that is emblematic of his father, John Romita Sr.) offered a contemporary flare to the book that bridged the mainstream/underground comics schism that was alive and well at the time. Additionally, Romita's frequent use of abstract, asymmetric panel layouts was the first such undertaking to appear in *UXM* since Neal Adams's legendary run on the book, pushing the series once again toward consistent visual experimentation. Thus, where Smith's line art pointed toward soft sophistication, Romita's pointed toward a differently mature sensibility, one that Claremont seized upon and reflected in his own storytelling.

Beyond the contribution of the visual team, this era of Claremont's *X-Men* was greatly enhanced by the various editorial personnel with whom he interacted. A concise summary of this is provided by Marvel editor in chief Jim Shooter, who offers his top-down perspective on Claremont's relationships with his editors,

Figure 5. "He'll Never Make Me Cry" (*Uncanny X-Men*, vol. 1, no. 183). Art by John Romita Jr. and Dan Green. John Romita Jr., penciller.

providing some intriguing insight into the nature of their collaboration and what each offered to the working dynamic between creative and editorial:

> I mean, [Roger] Stern was very good. [Jim] Salicrup was pretty good. Then he had Louise [Simonson], and then he had Ann [Nocenti] who was trained by Louise. He had the A-Team. So, I didn't have to get involved too much but I would, occasionally. Where the editor would come to me and say, "What do you think of this?" or show me something. But at any rate, I'd find stuff and then I'd get into arguments with Chris. He'd want to do something and I'd say, "I don't think it's a good idea." And with me he'd argue. If Louise said, "Chris, do it." He would do it. He was afraid of Louise; he wasn't afraid of me. But yeah, he really worked really well with Ann and Louise. They really knew how to get the best out of him. (n.p.)

Simonson was a rare woman in a male-dominated industry. She credits being thick-skinned and determined as the keys to her ability to break through the industry's gender barrier, though she also credits Jim Shooter for his willingness to hire female editors: "There were people who were appalled at the idea of me getting anywhere near the *real* Marvel books: the Fantastic Four, the Avengers, that stuff. I know of one or two people who just didn't think women belonged anywhere near the core titles" (qtd. in Riesman n.p.). As perhaps the most definitive editor on the Claremont run, however, Simonson was deeply sympatico with Claremont's work, creating a seamless later transition for her to begin writing within the X-Universe and contributing to highly integrated crossovers that redefined the industry. How she got to that role speaks, simply, to Shooter's assessment of being effective with the writer she was assigned to edit: "I was told that Chris was considered difficult to work with and they thought that for some reason he would work well with me" (qtd. in DeFalco 137). Along the way, Simonson wrote iconic storylines such as Magik's

"Inferno" tragedy in the pages of *New Mutants* and Angel's transition to Archangel in the pages of *X-Factor*. She also created (or cocreated) a number of lucrative Marvel intellectual properties, including Cable, Power Pack, Rictor, and Apocalypse, all within the same shared universe as Claremont.

When Simonson transitioned from editor to writer, Ann Nocenti took over as Claremont's editor. From 1984 to 1988, Nocenti provided a unique skill set to complement Claremont at a time when *Uncanny X-Men* had established itself as Marvel's best-selling title despite catastrophic departures and narrative experimentation. Nocenti was highly educated, politically outspoken, and deeply gifted as a storyteller in her own right (as evidenced by her later, much-loved run on *Daredevil*). All of these talents accentuated Claremont's storytelling throughout the mid-1980s, evolving the series in compelling ways.

With a (largely) new team of collaborators in place, Claremont continued to explore in-depth relationship mechanics in this era, taking the superhero comic to a place that is almost antithetical to the concept of superhero comics as masculinist power fantasies aimed at adolescent boys. On the pages themselves, Claremont further rejuvenated the series with new characters or new characterizations of existing ones.

A central example of this is Magneto, the first villain faced by the original X-Men and a character who is emblematic of the mustache-twirling megalomaniacs populating Marvel Comics in the 1960s and 1970s.[1] As mentioned previously, the Magneto that we see in *God Loves, Man Kills* is sympathetic and sensible but Claremont would adopt a similar approach in the ongoing *X-Men* series by portraying him as a man whose evil tendencies were born from Holocaust trauma. "It appeared to me that a character as extreme as Magneto had to be anchored to a devastating history. His rage and violence had to be rooted in a believable historic context" ("No Straw Dogs Here" 8). This retcon was received quite favorably, with scholar Marie-Catherine Caillava noting, "Magneto's being a Jew is of paramount importance. It defines the very relationship between reality and fiction" (99) by connecting the character's identity and the history that formed it to the real-world experiences of the readers. Charlotte F. Werbe notes that one particular issue of the series (*UXM* #161, which explores Magneto's work at an Israeli hospital for Holocaust survivors) "not only echoes, but also anticipates the academic and popular lexicon of trauma current in the 1980s and 1990s" (n.p.). Werbe further describes how *UXM* #161 is prescient in portraying the lingering impacts of Holocaust trauma on its victims and reflects a broader engagement with the subject that was simultaneously occurring in more respected media forms: "Dori Laub's 'Holocaust Survivors: Adaptation to Trauma,' published only a few years before *Uncanny X-Men* 161, enumerates many of the symptoms Holocaust survivors experience, including 'a continuing sense of responsibility of the dead, which serves to keep them psychologically alive'; 'the inevitable and utter loneliness beneath such restitutive attempts'; and 'grief, loss, hopelessness and helplessness,' ultimately stressing the way that trauma 'severely [taxes] ego capacities'" (Laub n.p.).

Aligning this sense of responsibility to the dead with Magneto's mission toward all mutants makes for a particularly compelling connection between his trauma and his mission—instantly casting the iconic villain into an entirely different, and quite tragic, light. As Claremont notes, "With Magneto, he's still climbing the ladder and dealing with the mistakes he's made. He's trying to get better. That, for me, is a conflict with a sort of Shakespearean balance" ("I'm Chris Claremont" n.p.).

Magneto's transition from irredeemable villain to antihero would form the centerpiece of *Uncanny X-Men* in the bicentennial issue #200, in which Claremont literally has the villain answer for his crimes at The Hague. Claremont's personal judgment of the character is made quite clear by the end of the issue, when Charles Xavier—unable to fulfill his post as mentor of the X-Men, leaves Magneto in charge of his young students ("The Trial of Magneto!"), effectively validating the perspective that Magneto is (and perhaps was always) a virtuous and trustworthy man who simply lost his way.

We can find a quite similar thread in the introduction of the new X-Men character, Rogue, the first new mainstay on the team since the introduction of Kitty Pryde. Rogue debuts in *Avengers Annual* #10 (written by Claremont) as the ward and child soldier of the villain Mystique. Rogue's powers allow her to absorb the psyche and superpowers of any character that she makes flesh-to-flesh contact with. Driven to near madness by these powers, she abandons her mother and seeks refuge with the X-Men, who seem on the brink of rejecting her out of loyalty to the friends that Rogue had assaulted previously (most notably Carol Danvers), but Charles Xavier refuses to waiver in his mission to help all mutants and Rogue is, begrudgingly, accepted by her teammates.

What follows with the character is an extended arc of redemption that explores the concept of restorative justice. Her atonement arc throughout the run focuses on a great number of key elements of the restorative justice process, such as collaboration and reintegration rather than isolation from the people she has hurt. We see this explored very directly through Rogue's joining the X-Men and her gradual reintegration into the community after her role within the Brotherhood of Evil Mutants under the leadership of Mystique. Restorative justice also focuses on exploration of unintended consequences, and indeed Rogue is made to see the full extent of the damage of her actions—the people she's hurt, the communities she's fractured, the second- and third-tier effects. Finally, restorative justice focuses on respecting all parties in a crime—victim, offender, community, and so on—and thus we can see the importance of Xavier's vision in contrast to others. Most of the team would happily cast her out, but X is capable of seeing her as worthy of redemption.

In addition to restorative justice, the character offers a lot of potential to explore contemporary sexual politics with regard to women's bodily agency. Comics scholar Michael Campochiaro writes, "Women's bodies and their choices regarding them are simultaneously admired, objectified, and legislated by men. I think Rogue can be seen as a metaphor for all of that" (n.p.). Early on, Rogue's body is characterized consistently as out of control and dangerous and, perhaps more importantly, exploited for its power by forces outside of her control, a problem that actually persists once she joins Xavier's X-Men. The emphasis on flesh-to-flesh contact without consent and including kissing in her superpower methodology lends itself to sexual symbolism. At the same time, Rogue's power prevents her from expressing her own sexual agency—she is unable to touch people that she might be attracted to for fear of injuring them.

Rogue is often rendered in an androgynous light through dress and hairstyle (by 1980s standards) and later through the additional superpowers that she siphons from Carol Danvers (including superstrength and invulnerability). Thus, like many Claremont heroines, she has the potential to queer gender roles. Speaking of this potential in "Flesh to Flesh Contact: Marvel Comics' Rogue and the Queer Feminist Imagination," Anthony Michael D'Agostino makes an intriguing case for the queer connotations embedded in Rogue within her initial depiction:

> Rogue's distinctive original character design visually ratifies her engagement with lesbian feminist values as articulated in "The Woman Identified Woman." Her brown hair, streaked with white is closely cropped, giving her a distinctly masculine appearance. And unlike most superheroines and female supervillains, whose skintight and revealing costumes purposefully invite the heterosexual male gaze, Rogue's head-to-toe green jumpsuit, detailed with folds and creases to mark loose fit, de-emphasize her breasts and hips closing her body off from that gaze. Rogue is coded as masculine, even butch, flirting with stereotypes of lesbianism. (262)

Of course, Rogue would later undertake a complex visual transformation that would see her grow long hair and don a swimsuit-inspired, skintight costume that accentuates her breasts and hips, seemingly resubjecting her to the male gaze by the terms of this argument. D'Agostino further argues, "Although Rogue is consistently characterized as heterosexual in her object choice, as the daughter of Mystique and her lesbian partner in crime and lover, Destiny, Rogue is, in her own way, lesbian identified" (262). This aspect stays the same throughout the run, as does Rogue's occupation of a traditionally male role on the team (powerhouse brawler), but it's interesting to consider how and why the character might have shed these queer signifiers over the course of Claremont's time on the book. All of this is to say that Rogue is a symbolically dense, versatile character, one that readers can project a wide array of sex, gender, and bodily concepts upon, thanks to a richness of metaphorical potential in all of these lights.

Another new X-person with a number of queer signifiers in this same time period is Rachel Summers, who Claremont describes as "a stand-in for all the children of the world who have lived through fierce trauma and have to find a way to move forward" ("A Lost Soul" 312). Rachel's visual representation (an embrace of new wave eighties fashion) can be seen to signify not just 1980s fashion but also an emergent perspective on human sexuality that was seeping into the mainstream during this time period. Through these signifiers, Rachel is able to embody within Marvel Comics an entire subculture, one that holds the capacity to challenge sexual norms of the time while also advocating for the relinquishment of gender and sexual binaries.

At the narrative level, Rachel creates a compelling extension of "The Dark Phoenix Saga" by presenting a second human host for the Phoenix, one with a compelling backstory and a unique connection to key Claremontian themes such as predestination and liminality. In an interview, Claremont suggests that he specifically brings the character in for this purpose of revisiting the Phoenix's path: "That has a meaning and that's why I brought in Rachel, who's trying to stand up for everything. Every point in the journey where Jean failed. And yet, she faces the same temptations, because she's a baby Phoenix and she's learning" ("I'm Chris Claremont").

Rachel's first appearance in the "Days of Future Past" storyline, years prior, is brief yet oddly portentous of what's to come for her in this era. In just a few panels of presence, Rachel is made to experience the death of all of her remaining loved ones (via telepathic link), left to hideout in a ruined world, and it is Rachel who delivers the grim speculation that the actions of the time traveler in the past might not right the future at all. They might just create a new timeline. Three years later, Rachel would return to the X-Universe and to the Earth-616 timeline as a mysterious figure with a traumatic past. This too would establish a theme of Rachel's character moving forward—someone who is constantly found in a state of recuperation from an unspoken, off-panel story that is only revealed incrementally, one snippet at a time.

This combination of unspoken trauma and mystery makes Rachel an ideal vehicle for Claremont's go-to characterization strategy: torturing the characters emotionally in order to make them sympathetic to the reader and to enhance their heroic character by giving them every right to be downright unheroic, if they should so choose. The greatest torture provided to Rachel is the cultivation of her backstory as someone who does not and should not exist in this timeline. She comes to realize that the timeline she's in does not even connect to hers, displacing her from the very concept of past and future. She was unable to alter her reality and is forever excised from any sense of continuity. Her character arc then becomes a story of self-definition in the absence of these external forces, giving her a drive toward agency that mirrors that of the original Phoenix, Jean Grey, while at the same time giving her a sense of simmering anger, self-hatred, and isolation—just like that of Jean Grey but when she became Dark Phoenix specifically. Even among the found family of the X-Men, Rachel cannot simply move forward anew, yet she is largely unwilling to address her past, fearing the emotional burden she places on others.

Importantly, Rachel succeeds as the Phoenix but fails as a superhero, ultimately succumbing to her own anger and death drive in consequence of her traumatic (and traumatizing) past. She can't simply "get over it," especially given her own self-imposed isolation from those who would be her found family. She loses control and attempts to commit the murder of a supervillain, only to be stabbed by Wolverine in a somewhat bizarre attempt to defend the values of heroism. It's a perplexing end to her story in *UXM*, but when Rachel drags her dying, bleeding out body away from her found family, it is obviously tragic. Never before in the pages of *X-Men* comics had any character been so completely and utterly alone.

Rachel's story was meant to pick up from there in a miniseries that never came to fruition. Instead, she reemerges in Claremont's *Excalibur* (discussed in a later chapter), reborn (because Phoenix) as a confident and assertive hero. It is here that Phoenix is finally redeemed, with Rachel eschewing the corruptions of power and temptations of revenge in favor of a selfless and altruistic purpose. It would get more complicated from there with Claremont's departure from Marvel, and even with his eventual return—to torture Rachel even further—but viewed holistically, Rachel's story is one of legacy, taking on the mantle of her inheritance and with it the burden of atonement. If the Phoenix Saga ends with the death of Jean Grey, it remains an epic tale of tragedy and triumph. If we read it as continuing forward with Rachel, however, it can be seen to take on new dimensions and nuances.

In a similarly expanded reading, Claremont's long game storytelling strategies can likewise be seen in his ongoing development of Kitty in this era, which signals the development of a fascinating reader surrogate, one that is able to trade upon the sense of mortality created by the death of Jean Grey in "The Dark Phoenix Saga." Scholar Carol Cooper notes the following (for both Kitty and Storm):

> But watching how a combination of emotional instability and increasing power slowly corrupted a female teammate long thought beyond the possibility of corruption left a lasting impression on Storm and Kitty. It understandably scared them to realize that either of them could fall prey to the same kind of corruption.

Storm—the older and wiser of the two—understood her case was already different than Jean's and struggled to explain that difference to Kitty, who must logically prepare to undergo similar tests of strength and character on her own one day. (193)

Thus, Kitty's character development (in terms of both her relationship with Storm and her function as a reader surrogate) informs and is informed by the continuity that Claremont is working within, creating a complex resonance that looks both backward and forward in the *X-Men* timeline to create a richer tapestry of narrative depth.

We can see this haunting shadow of Jean's death manifest quite prominently in a storyline known as "the Brood Saga" (*Uncanny X-Men* #156–67). Where "Dark Phoenix" moves toward a cohesive metaphor, "the Brood Saga" instead offers variations on a theme—that of mortality, approaching this issue from multiple angles based on individual character experiences surrounded by obvious death symbols. For Kitty the story is about mortal consciousness and the fear of death as a motivating force. The Brood (parasitic aliens with the capacity to transform humans into mindless aliens themselves) force her to contemplate her life, the things she wants to accomplish, even spurring her to rush her (age-inappropriate) relationship with Colossus. In all aspects, the main theme is death, but Kitty's youth and naivety juxtaposed with the recent demise of Jean Grey creates an intimate sense of vulnerability that then extends to the rest of the team, enriching their symbolic encounters with mortality as well and allowing Claremont to craft a rich and, frankly, underrated narrative about living in the shadow of death.

As mentioned, the Brood Saga accelerates Kitty's ongoing age-inappropriate romance with Colossus, another key character development in this era and one that might represent a noteworthy inversion of gendered tropes in comics. When perceived from the perspective of Colossus, the Kitty/Piotr relationship can be read as inappropriate, uncomfortable, or even predatory, but if approached via Kitty it can be seen as a gender-inverted representation of a common fantasy construct. Romanticizing a relationship between a nineteen-year-old man and a fourteen- to fifteen-year-old girl can hold the potential to validate patriarchal perceptions of underage girls that can make them even more vulnerable to exploitation, especially when Piotr reciprocates her feelings. Kitty is not, however, an object within the pages of *X-Men* comics. She is a key identification figure with the potential to enact romantic fantasies of the readership rather than simply functioning as a passive object for the fantasies of the reader. The idea that a young woman experiencing puberty would develop a crush on an older boy with a Mister Universe musculature, an artist's soul, and a hero's heart is not at all hard to imagine, and Piotr can be seen as a wish fulfillment figure in that sense. Notably, most major romantic milestones between the two characters are portrayed from Kitty's point of view—featuring far more of her thought processes than Piotr's and within stories that are advanced, almost exclusively, through Kitty's actions and decisions—her agency. To the other men on the team, Kitty forms equally important relationships, including a key mentorship with Wolverine (who even supports the idea of Kitty leading the X-Men) and a heartwarming platonic friendship with Nightcrawler.

Apart from Kitty, the other character taking center stage in the run to an increasing degree is Storm, who becomes leader during Cyclops's departure. In accord with this singular achievement, Claremont and team develop Ororo's character to greater depths in this era through a number of life-altering events. The first is murder. In "Dancin' in the Dark" from *UXM* #170, Storm is backed into a corner and has to fight a duel to the death with the Morlock leader Callisto in order to save her teammates. We are assured by Nightcrawler (acting as a reader surrogate), that Storm is incapable of taking a life. He is (and we as readers are) wrong, however. Superhero comics are famous for advocating the existence of moral absolutes in the pursuit of justice, but Storm takes that idea of the "one rule" and stabs it in the chest of her persecutor, Callisto.[2] The consequences of this action are steep for

Figure 6. Storm stabs Callisto in "Dancin' in the Dark" (*Uncanny X-Men*, vol. 1, no. 170). Paul Smith, penciller.

Storm as a character, reflecting a more mature perspective on the burden of leadership, while operating consistently with Storm's sense of martyrdom and indomitable will. It's a shocking move for her, but not out of character when one stops to consider it.

The shock value of her choice is enhanced through a number of facets: Storm's femininity (highly stereotyped in 1980s comics), her harmonious existence with nature, her genial and polite demeanor, and her emotional empathy all speak against the act of killing. And that's kind of the point. Through it, the reader is made to identify with Callisto, who learns too late that Storm's entire strategy hinged on her opponent assuming she was too decent to use lethal force. Like Callisto, we underestimated Ororo. Thus, the message that the action sent was clear to both readers and the other X-Men: Storm will do whatever it takes to succeed. At the same time, however, the horrified reaction of her teammates symbolizes the understanding that morality is a privilege in Claremont's world, not a virtue. Kurt even admonishes her for her actions, unaware, perhaps, of the charity that Storm has extended him in taking on the grim but necessary action herself. He had volunteered for the duel, but Storm replaced him, identifying the burden as belonging to the X-Men's leader alone. In the aftermath of the battle, Storm weighs her individual values against family obligation. Claremont further symbolizes her descent as she loses control of her weather powers and annihilates her beloved plants. A few issues later, she gets rid of them entirely. This character arc focused on the traumatic burden of leadership will continue throughout Claremont's run, surfacing prominently in the "Mutant Massacre" and "Fall of the Mutants," with Storm frequently left to contemplate the extent to which her personal ideals have been compromised by her role as leader.

The second life-altering event is love. In "Scarlet in Glory" from *UXM* #172, Storm has a subtextual love affair with the androgynous ronin character, Yukio, resulting in an epiphany and a radical shift in her attitude and appearance, ushering in Storm's so-called punk look, a shocking transition but one that had key representational impacts as well. "And when Storm sports the Mohawk and leather jacket, she creates an iconic representation for readers on the margins, both female and male" (Campochiaro).

The third life-altering event for Ororo is disempowerment at the literal level. Storm loses her powers when struck by a weapon designed by the mutant Forge. In horror at what his weapon has done, Forge takes Ororo into his home in order to help her recuperate and heal, leading to the now famous double-sized issue "Lifedeath: A Love Story." In the climax of "Lifedeath," Claremont and guest artist Barry Windsor-Smith use a deeply symbolic fantasy setting to help construct their metaphor for the real-world experience of panic and self-realization that can come when transitioning out of a toxic or abusive relationship. "Lifedeath" begins in a haunting state of absolute stillness, reflective of the deep depression that Ororo finds herself in. From there, the story follows Ororo's progressive opening up to her own vulnerability, but then the story quickly turns (as deceit is revealed) into a frantic-paced thriller. The frantic nature of the final scene is a poignant reflection of Ororo's confused state of mind. She's been through the ringer, so to speak, and though she's clearly right to distrust Forge, the dramatic irony of the scene is that the reader knows he does care for her as well. Her sense of betrayal is what's particularly heartbreaking about the scene. Ororo has been established in continuity as reserved, shy, and self-sacrificing. What she gave Forge was the kind of absolute trust and intimacy that she withholds from even those closest to her. He betrayed that. Watching Storm panic and start to question everything is thus harrowing. She confronts Forge (first with a left hook and second with sharp words): "You live in your high tower—untouched, untouchable—surrounded by illusion, so terrified of the real, living world you cannot bear to violate the sanctity of your space even with something as small as a flower. Your home is a true reflection of its creator" ("Lifedeath," n.p.). This speaks to the duality between them. Storm's connection to nature isn't just elemental: it's also a commitment to real lived experience, to truth and even a form of purity. Forge's aerie, and the holographic illusions it contains, are just fantasies. The final panel sees Storm walk away from Forge, committed to "another road" (n.p.). Again the setting is perfectly poignant, with Storm walking barefoot across broken glass (a difficult path) away from Forge, who is dumbstruck in the rain.

Under normal circumstances, a powerful and beloved female character losing their superpowers is a textbook example of Gail Simone's concept of fridging. But instead of using her disempowerment to realign Storm with hegemonic ideals (and making her Forge's powerless love interest), "Lifedeath" sets Storm on a course of self-actualization and empowerment, one that includes a pilgrimage to her mother's ancestral homelands and that eventually culminates in her return to the X-Men to battle Cyclops (the iconic alpha male X-Man) for leadership of the team in *UXM* #201. Despite having no superpowers, she wins.

That same issue showcases Claremont's emotional nuances as a writer of superhero soap opera through the portrayal of Cyclops, a character who has largely been absent from the series at this point. Immediately prior to his duel with Storm, he verbally duels his own wife, Madelyne Pryor, over his desire to stay with the X-Men in an exchange that features some of Claremont's most direct analysis of Cyclops's character hang-ups. Before this, Madelyne expresses her building frustration to Ororo. Storm tells her, "He is a very private man. Such feelings are hard for him to face, much less reveal. But they are there, Madelyne. He does love you very much" (4). Madelyne isn't convinced. The debate scene in question begins with Cyclops's declaration to Madelyne: "I have to stay. To lead them." Madelyne, who has her own career as a pilot, calls him on the implicit misogyny of his presumption that she should stay with their child. "What about me? I have a life of my own—a career—do you expect me to chuck it?!" Cyclops then makes it clear that he absolutely did expect that. Madelyne responds that a child is a shared responsibility between partners and even takes the conversation into the territory of financial earning potential: "I have skills, I can earn a living—can you say the same?!" In her frustration, Madelyne then effectively psychoanalyzes Scott: "Is your life so hollow—your sense of self-worth so fragile—that you believe you're nothing without them? What about me, what about us? My commitment supersedes everything—are you telling me the same doesn't hold true in reverse" (13)? Cyclops has no response, and the pair hover in a beautifully rendered silence by guest artists Rick Leonardi and Whilce Portacio, with Glynis Oliver still on colors (figure 7). The punctuating image features an unnecessary separation of panels between them to signify the distance that has now formed within their marriage. It's a scene that adds emotional heft to the duel that follows (and the choices that inform it), while advancing the inherent conflict between Cyclops's sense of duty and self as well as the fundamental inequity emerging in his relationship with Madelyne and thus the sheer complexity and nuances of the soap opera that Claremont was building behind the veneer of a conventional gods-in-tights monomyth.

Perhaps the boldest subversion in this era, however, is a storyline called "The Mutant Massacre" from *Uncanny X-Men* #210–13 and the aftermath it created.[3] Claremont had been spinning his X-Men narrative for a decade at this point, but was still quite content, noting that, "I discovered I was in no way interested in giving up the title—I was having *far* too much fun. I became increasingly fascinated by the characters' motivations. I wanted to know what made them tick" ("No Straw Dog Here" 8). In pursuing this inquiry, Claremont's main strategy in the "Mutant Massacre" is elegantly simple: knock the characters and the reader off-balance by deviating from expectations to put them in the characters' shoes. The villains in the story are a (mostly) unknown entity. Their arrival is barely foreshadowed, and they aren't even seen, except in silhouette, until it's already far too late to stop the massacre from occurring. This timing is important. We are not forewarned of their coming (except in a very general sense), and the X-Men are not presented with a trial by which they might stop them, thus deviating from the typical protagonist/antagonist structure that

Figure 7. Cyclops and Madelyne in "Duel" (*Uncanny X-Men*, vol. 1, no. 201). Rick Leonardi, penciller.

Marvel Comics relies upon. Furthermore, the villains embody contradictory principles: they are hunting down and killing mutants, but they are themselves mutants (hence the cognitive dissonance). Their motivations are unclear and will not be resolved for years.

The level and nature of the violence is genuinely shocking—*X-Men* was dark at the time, but never this brutal. That creates more dissonance—"how is this happening in an X-Men book?"—which again reflects the same perspective of the team, who are unaccustomed to this type of traumatic brutality. This might seem contradictory for a book that has more than one genocide under its belt already, but this is where execution becomes paramount over content alone. The violence is depicted in scenes here that would normally not be shown on panel. This gets enhanced by the concept of plot armor. The Morlocks are a (mostly) benign underclass of mutant refugees under the protection of Storm herself. They aren't the nameless and faceless aliens who appear in one page only to die in "The Dark Phoenix Saga." Readers know these people. Ultimately, the heroes are quickly dismantled to an absurd degree that sees three core X-Men taken off the team in immediate succession (all from injuries suffered in a single battle). The combined effect is, of course, shock and awe, but that is what the X-Men themselves experience diegetically, and thus the audience is situated very much in the heroes' perspective, creating a relatable viewpoint that helps sell the entire story.

Coming out of this storyline, the Claremont run then shifts the dominant theme of the series from that of control to that of resolve in the face of progressively overwhelming forces. The atrocity of the massacre (coming right on the heels of Rachel's tragic departure) signals the transition to an even darker X-Universe but also devastates the team to an unparalleled degree with the loss of Kurt, Kitty, and Piotr. From there, the X-Men are left in a rare position of pragmatic necessity, desperately forming a new team and radically reconsidering the nature of their mission, purpose, and even their values. Piece by piece they become disconnected from their home, their families, and even their very lives.

In the wake of the mutant massacre, Claremont tries out new X-Men (Longshot, Dazzler, and Psylocke), a new direction for the series, and even a new penciller, who would go on to redefine the franchise. Each of these new X-Men, along with returning X-Man, Havok, can be seen to represent abandoned characters from outside the mainline X-Men franchise. Longshot was a character created by a pair of Claremont friends/collaborators: writer Ann Nocenti and artist Arthur Adams. He was originally created as part of Nocenti's allegorical commentary on media saturation and values in a self-titled miniseries, but Claremont was able to absorb him (along with a number of Nocenti/Adams characters) into the mainline X-Universe despite some notable tonal inconsistencies, with Nocenti describing Longshot as having a "silly, naïve buoyancy" (n.p.) that runs contrary to the grimness of the rest of the characters in the cast at this time.

Similarly, Dazzler began as one of the most ambitious transmedia experiments in comics history. When she failed, Claremont reclaimed her and integrated her into the X-Men universe by decentralizing her and drawing out her relationships to other X-Men.[4] Here, Claremont picked her up and wove her into X-Men. Where other narratives had focused on the Mary Sue aspects of Dazzler, Claremont's Alison was paralyzed by self-doubt, soft, and simply in way over her head as a superhero, both in terms of ability and in terms of desire to be one. From there Claremont cultivated an existing rivalry with Rogue, a romance with Longshot, a friendship with the other X-women, and a shared misery/rivalry with the other reluctant X-Man, Havok. At the same time, Alison contributed verve and style to an otherwise grim and downtrodden new team.

Psylocke was a character created by Claremont in the pages of *Captain Britain*, who was then completely reimagined (right down to the hair color) by later *Captain Britain* authors. Where Claremont is famous for the character rehabilitation of Carol Danvers in the wake of a character assassination (in *Avengers* #200), he does something quite similar for Psylocke after an unfortunate and similarly offensive narrative depiction. Claremont created Betsy in *Captain Britain* #8 (1976) and made her a pilot (like Claremont's mother once again). When he left the book, Betsy fell into the capable hands of writers such as Jamie Delano, Alan Moore, and Alan Davis. In one notable story from *Captain Britain* vol. 2, #13 ("It's Hard to Be a Hero"), written and drawn by Alan Davis, Betsy would briefly take on the mantle of Captain Britain herself, only to be brutally beaten and have her eyes gouged out by a villain called Slaymaster. The story is titled "It's Hard to Be a Hero" and is the first writing credit for Davis on *Captain Britain* (a title he'd been illustrating for some time). Davis would go on to become a very talented and accomplished writer, but this issue features a textbook example of fridging. Betsy takes on a traditionally masculine role and is immediately humiliated and put in place. Her maiming is used at the narrative level to incentivize her brother, and the brutal violence that Betsy is subjected to ultimately leads to her depowering. Claremont then reclaims and rehabilitates Psylocke less than a year after her blinding. In *New Mutants Annual* #2 (illustrated by Alan Davis), Psylocke is given back her sight and her sense of purpose, and she is even allowed to outshine her brother (who also appears) before finding her place in the X-Universe ("Why Do We Do These Things We Do?"). From there, Claremont establishes Betsy as a 100 percent valid and legitimate hero—if anything, she's seen to have an excess of the heroic spirit, and, through this depiction, the character can move beyond a rough turn in the character's history to become an elite Marvel superhero.

The development of the new X-Men builds toward something of a resolution and transition to a new era with another underappreciated storyline titled "The Fall of the Mutants" in 1988 (*UXM* #225–27). Where "Mutant Massacre" and "Inferno" have received a lot of attention as iconic *UXM* crossover events, there's something to be said for the surreal and dissonant event that is "Fall of the Mutants," an ambitious and experimental arc that thrives on chaos. It doesn't shock status quo the way "Mutant Massacre" does, and it doesn't culminate the way the later "Inferno" story does (discussed in the next chapter). "Fall of the Mutants" exists in a somewhat formless postmassacre, preinferno space. In a very strange way, that's quite appropriate for a story arc that brings together different mythologies, religions, villains, timelines, and universes. The team itself is still in turmoil—a mixture of mainstays and untested new additions. Kurt and Kitty are still too injured to participate, but Colossus returns. Obviously, this level of instability and confusion requires virtuoso imagery to ground it, sell it, and make it compelling, and the visual team of Marc Silvestri on pencils and Dan Green on inks are right at the top of their game, crafting lavish, surreal landscapes and tumultuous battlefields. The story has some important pieces to it: a test of heroic virtue through martyrdom, a new allyship with a divine being, the return of Storm's powers, the dark origin of Forge, a tense reunion between Rogue and Mystique, and more. My point in all of this is that "Fall of the Mutants" is a piece of chaotic but compelling storytelling that—somehow—brings an engagingly formless era of the book to a close and ushers in a new definition of what the series would become in the Outback age—the subject of a later chapter.

CHAPTER FOUR

Mutant Mitosis

The X Spin-Offs

> I've always looked at comics as a seduction. The readers aren't here to fall in love with the exploits but with the characters—who in turn are defined by the world around them, the adventures they undergo and most importantly of all, how they interact with their companions—and adversaries—along the way.
> —Chris Claremont ("A Lost Soul" 312)

When Chris Claremont began his run on *X-Men* comics, there was one, and only one, *X-Men* series and its survival was by no means guaranteed. In the years that have since passed, there have been close to 200 *X-Men* spin-off series and over 700 one-shots and limited series. As much as this reflects the success of the franchise, it also reflects important market forces, and, during the 1980s, Claremont found himself placed in a uniquely challenging position within the enduring intersection of art and commerce at Marvel Comics.

The 1970s witnessed a shift from mass-market and newsstand distribution to the direct market in which retailers purchased their comics on a no-returns system. As scholar Derek Johnson notes, "With retailers eating the cost of unsold titles, the market for content contracted, with only those titles which retailers felt confident they could sell reaching the shelves" (17). This meant that name recognition and intellectual property suddenly became much more important than in prior years. As Johnson describes, this also created a "zero sum game" (17), where selling a new Marvel title to a retailer could (in theory) result in said retailer purchasing one less DC comic to sell to their consumers, and thus Marvel could help itself while hurting the competition through expansion. This franchise strategy of expansion, therefore, emerged in the 1980s as a negotiation of direct market conflicts. But how expansion impacted Claremont's work on *UXM* is hard to say. While it certainly increased the visibility of the broader franchise and expanded the canvas that Claremont and team had to work with, it could also be seen to dilute the overall impact of the series and to create some internal conflicts in the storytelling.

And indeed, this was Claremont's concern about spin-offs: "He thought it would dilute the intensity of *X-Men*. Chris loved the book, and he loved his characters almost like they were real people. He really wanted the best for them" (Simonson qtd. in DeFalco 139). Claremont's resistance to expansion was inevitably overruled in consequence of Marvel's need to leverage the success of its X-Men to create new titles. Not wanting to lose creative control of his story, Claremont was forced to take on writing duties for these new titles. "If there was a mandate for a new mutant-related spin-off, the notoriously proprietary Claremont would take a deep breath, look at his schedule, and figure out a way to do it himself" (Howe 286).

This process starts, arguably, with the 1982 Wolverine miniseries that Douglas Wolk describes as "a stark, gorgeous, violent thing that indulged *Daredevil* artist Frank Miller's enthusiasm for drawing Japanese landscapes (and ninja attacks)" (159). This partnership began somewhat inauspiciously with Claremont trapped in traffic in a vehicle with his then friend and rival, Miller:

> I really wanted to do something with Frank, and conveniently I had a car. I was taking him and some people up the PCH from San Diego to L.A. where we were going to a post-Con event. And somewhere along the way we got caught in a huge tailback (which is to say, a

traffic jam.) . . . but we're sitting there, and I just started pitching the story. Frank goes "eh, I don't want to draw a story of this guy hacking and stabbing people for four issues" and I said "that's all right, neither do I." Then both of us started talking about Japanese culture and philosophy and Frank really loved it, and I really loved it, and Logan really loved it. ("I'm Chris Claremont" n.p.)

Once brought to fruition, the miniseries launched with an iconic six-page intro story that immediately established who Logan is, the duality that defined him, and his capacity to symbolize and disrupt perceptual boundaries between animal and person. This intro (about a renegade bear) establishes the fundamental theme of the series: the conflict between the primal and the civilized, with particular emphasis on destabilizing the distinction between the two of them by portraying the violence of civility as well as the nobility of the primal.

The grizzly encounter ("I Am Wolverine") demonstrates this principle perfectly. The bear is terrifying and deadly, but only because of the interference of man. A good comparison might be to Grendel, with Logan thereby cast in the Beowulf role. The literal story is simple: Wolverine hunts down and kills a rogue man-eating grizzly. He discovers that the bear only turned lethal when poisoned by a hunter, so Logan tracks the hunter and confronts him in a pub. Like the bear, the hunter showcases the destabilization of primal versus civilized; he used advanced technology to hunt the bear, but he lacked the nobility to finish the job, and people died in consequence. And so, Wolverine must hunt him down as well. Claremont and Miller use parallel form to establish this equivalence with some page symmetry featuring Wolverine in the top left corner descending both into the bear's den and into the bar that houses the unscrupulous hunter (figure 8). Additionally, the vignette clearly establishes the duality of Logan himself. He feels grief for killing the bear, but he also smiles when it first attacks him. He obeys the law in apprehending the hunter, but is delighted

Figure 8. Wolverine and the Bear from "I'm Wolverine" (*Wolverine*, vol. 1, no. 1). Frank Miller, penciller.

when the hunter chooses violence. Perhaps most importantly, the story also establishes Wolverine's unique position as a figure who can traverse through both worlds—primal and civilized—delivering justice in both and easily permeating the boundary between worlds that others simply cannot. It's a straightforward story, but it lays important groundwork for the miniseries that follows, defining the character arc that will accompany Logan's solo journeys for decades to follow as well. This opening then serves as a microcosm for the broader miniseries, which uses the trappings of feudal Japanese culture to push Wolverine into sober self-reflection about the nature of his own internal capacities for both violence and nobility.

By the early 1980s *Uncanny X-Men* had become quite dark and Marvel wanted a junior X-Men book—something child friendly to help diversify the audience, and Claremont obliged, despite reservations. First launched through a Marvel graphic novel in 1982, *The New Mutants* was a youth-oriented title that introduced a series of new young mutant characters to the Marvel lineup. Claremont's approach to youth orientation, however, was neither condescending nor sanitized. His kids existed in the same dark world of the mutant metaphor that surrounded the X-Men. If anything, their journey was harder due to their youthful naivety. The author notes:

> This *is* a book about racism, about people whose only "crime" is that they're different from the mainstream society around them. . . . These books have a special responsibility. They can speak to an audience that's forming its opinions, shaping its views of the world. It isn't a matter of preaching, it *is* a matter of showing—in as up front and personal a way as possible—what it means to be the object of prejudice. To walk the proverbial mile in the shoes of these kids. Who knows, if they come to understand how much hatred of this kind can hurt—if they can be made to see what it's like to be on the receiving end—perhaps they'll move beyond the need or impulse to dish it out. ("Introduction to New Mutants #45")

Though completely unquantifiable, this didactic function of *The New Mutants* is interesting to contemplate when considering Claremont's legacy. How many children became better human beings because of time spent with Illyana, Berto, Dani, and Doug?

In terms of reaching this younger audience, the power sets of the New Mutants characters all offer opportunities to speak very specifically to common experiences associated with pubescence. Wolfsbane has werewolf powers, reflecting hormonal urges (in-line with long-established werewolf symbology). Karma's power is psychic manipulation, offering some potential for symbolic representations of emotional manipulation common to teens. Mirage's power, meanwhile, is connected to a different form of manipulation: the ability to emotionally wound people by confronting them with their greatest fears and shame. This forces her to confront the consequences of private boundaries and social integration. Sunspot and Cannonball both offer the potential to speak to masculine pubescence—Bobby with nonsustainable bursts of violent physicality while Sam can be invulnerable so long as he's being outwardly aggressive (blastin'). Magik's dark magic (juxtaposed with a blue-eyed, blonde little girl appearance) offers a poignant reflection on the artificial nature of the extreme idealism that is heaped on teen girls, specifically, and the damaging nature of forcing them to live up to a prescribed gender role of innocence, domesticity, and fragility. Through these powers, *The New Mutants* characters are well suited to stories of awkward teen friendship/romance or to stories about mutants coming to terms and learning to control the bodily changes that are upturning their lives.

The series arguably hits its stride when Claremont is joined by Bill Sienkiewicz in issue #18 with the now famous "The Demon Bear Saga" storyline. Immediately, Sienkiewicz introduced a surreal style of artwork that was "as visually radical as anything that had ever appeared in pulp comics" (Wolk 160), artwork that would energize the book and redefine what popular comics illustration could do for decades to come. Sienkiewicz transitioned the New Mutants from "house style" visuals to a kind of innovative,

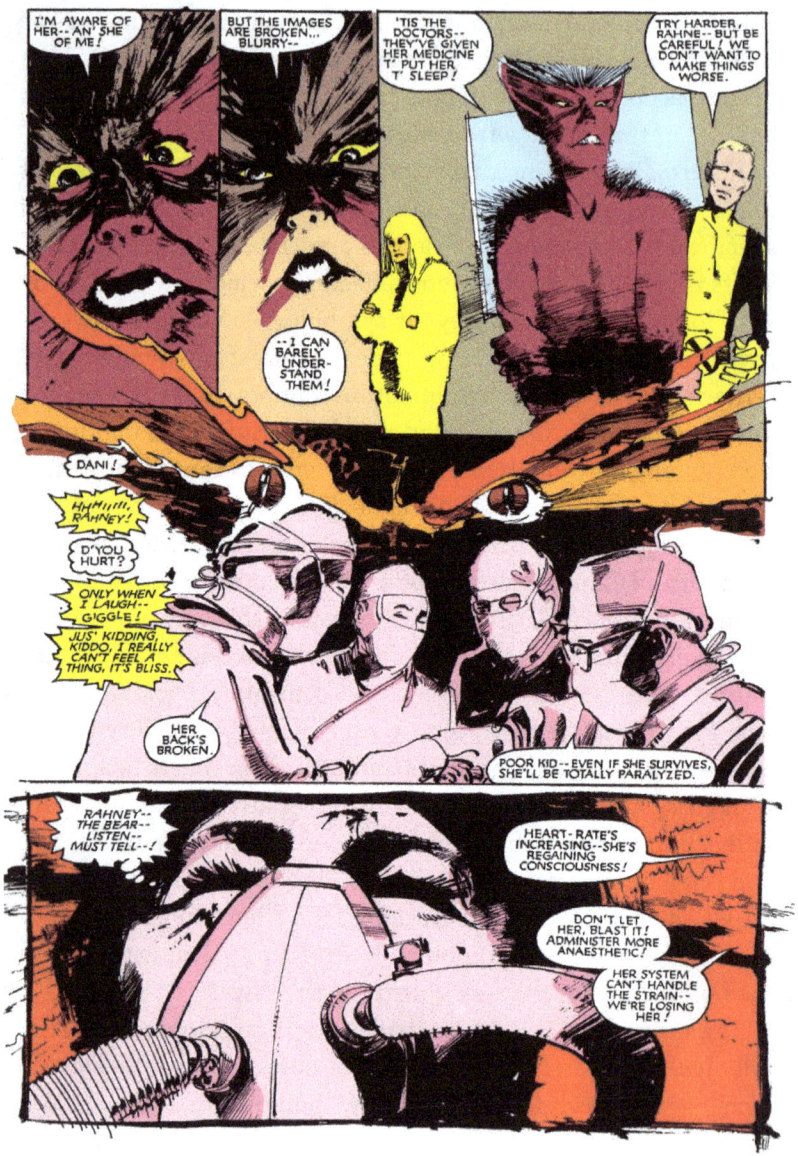

Figure 9. A Bill Sienkiewicz layout for "Siege" (*New Mutants*, vol. 1, no. 19). Bill Sienkiewicz, penciller.

mixed-media, experimental artwork that was rarely ever seen in Marvel Comics, and certainly not in a top-tier book. Sienkiewicz notes, "The thing I liked about it, it wasn't apathetic. It was polarizing. I tended to appreciate that. My big bugaboo is not so much work that's half-bad as much as work that's half-good, which to me is . . . playing it safe. In society it's just rampant. It's endemic to who we are now" (qtd. in CBR Staff n.p.). The results were buoying for the industry but also for Claremont specifically, who, empowered by Sienkiewicz's innovations, was able to lean hard away from the teen adventure serial, transitioning the book instead into surreal cosmic horror with an artist who could add a symbolic layer to each of Claremont's characters. "Because that's what Bill offers. When he puts pen to paper, a vision of the world and of the characters emerges. That is unlike any other creator I have ever seen. The thing with his tenure on New Mutants is he did not draw so much from text as subtext. . . . For a writer, that is the proverbial gold mine" ("I'm Chris Claremont" n.p.).

The arrival of Sienkiewicz also brought with it a darker tone for the series, one that Claremont responded to enthusiastically, pushing the book to new levels of existential terror and human suffering, themes that pervaded the series for the entirety of Claremont's run on it, even after Sienkiewicz's departure.

And indeed, the series features some of Claremont's best character work, particularly surrounding Magik (Illyana Rasputin), a subversive portrayal of post–sexual violence trauma whose metaphorical demons are personified through the haunting presence of literal demons and their persistent and exhausting threat to overwhelm her. Simply put, Illyana is a survivor and can function as a symbol of childhood sexual trauma—particularly the struggle to live with that kind of experience. The mapping of the allegory is subtle but consistent: Illyana is a young child, abducted to a hell dimension and forced into the servitude of an aggressive, possessive and abusive male patriarch.[1] The sexual violence is not explicit, but it is heavily implied, seen prominently through the violent sexual undertones of Limbo (such as its version of

Nightcrawler, presented as an aggressive sexual predator) and through the symbolism of lost souls and total possession through which the dimension operates. I should also note that though the sexual trauma was exclusively subtextual in the comic books, it was made textual for the recent *The New Mutants* film—a strong choice in a movie that didn't always make strong choices.[2]

When Illyana returns from her time in Limbo to rejoin the X-Men, from their perspective, she has lost her childhood, and they all have to adjust to this new version of Illyana while suffering through their own guilt at failing to protect her. This is nothing, however, compared to her suffering. Illyana carries Limbo with her in the form of her Darkchylde persona and soul sword. She finds herself striving to acclimate to a world that is incapable of reckoning with the experiences she has been through and, in some ways, with who she is now as a person. She hides her demonic powers out of fear and shame for how she would be received and for the effect that they have on her ability to integrate. All told, it's a horrifying burden to place on a teenager. Through Illyana, Claremont stages a complex and human portrayal of the all-too-common real-world experience of sexual trauma, one in which all manner of encounters can be seen to take on a symbolic resonance that speaks to a taboo subject in important ways. These all take a backseat, however, to the simplest possible truth of the character: Illyana is more than just a survivor of sexual abuse—she is a survivor of sexual abuse who is a superhero, one with a rare capacity to speak to and acknowledge her trauma without erasing it and without being wholly defined by it either. Thus, Claremont's Illyana again is an important representational milestone for Marvel Comics.

On a different representational note, Mirage (Dani Moonstar) is perhaps Claremont's most expansive (and, arguably, successful) portrayal of an Indigenous superhero. Like Storm before her, Dani becomes the leader of a superhero team and a key focal character with genuine narrative agency. Though overdetermined at times by her Indigeneity, Claremont shows a deft touch on that subject in a few key storylines, most notably in *New Mutants* #41 ("Way of the Warrior"), which presents Claremont's most robust consideration of Dani's Indigenous culture, using Dani's internal identity crisis to reflect upon the broader challenges of Indigeneity within a modern context, thus creating a rare, nuanced portrayal within a Western media that has a tendency to excise roughly 150 years of Indigenous experience, effectively fixing Indigenous characters in a precontact state that ignores the complex negotiations of Indigenous culture and identity within a modern world. Dani recounts how she experienced traditional Cheyenne learning with her grandfather, who also forced her to learn "the White man's schooling" despite Dani's hesitation (6). Her grandfather also notes that Dani's mother was a teacher. This creates conflict for Dani. Her heritage is Cheyenne, but her direct heritage through her mother itself points to the European style of education. Thus, she can't really choose one or the other without betraying some aspect of her familial legacy. She's trapped in a liminal space. At the mall that she finds built over a natural area she used to play in, she thinks, "I miss the land. But I love the stores" (9). Here Claremont gives Dani a deeply understandable affection for a symbol of modernity. Even while participating in this modern teenage ritual, Dani reflects "the White man and his way of life—won. Maybe that means it's better?" (10). She is again completely and totally conflicted and all of her internal anxieties reflect a broader cultural anxiety surrounding heritage versus assimilation.

Of course, Dani's sense of cultural affiliation is subject to external forces as well, such as the horrific racism that she's subject to at the hands of the people she grew up with. It's not simply a matter of which culture she likes best—acceptance and hostility factor in too. As Dani imagines challenging Death for the life of her childhood friend, her superpower forms Death into the image of a cowboy (18), the archetypal opponent of Indigenous people in the Western imaginary. When the real Death appears to console Dani later, it takes the form of an Indigenous elder (22). Claremont's representation of Dani's Indigeneity is imperfect in several ways, but issues such as this show a sincere and committed effort to engage with the subject in a modern context and with a humanizing approach to highly modern cultural anxieties faced by Indigenous youth.

The final bons mots to offer Claremont's characterization in his *The New Mutants* spin-off must go to the friendship he portrays between Cannonball (Sam Guthrie) and Sunspot (Roberto da Costa). In the pages of *The New Mutants*, Claremont cultivated Sam and 'Berto as one of Marvel's most enduring (and endearing) fraternal friendships by deeply integrating the friendship into each character's respective arc, allowing it to define them. Sam and Bobby are complete opposites. Sam is awkward, humble, and industrious, while Bobby is brash, confident, and entitled. Their friendship also transgresses social boundaries of economic class and race. Where many comics writers tend to establish friendships through forced statements, Claremont plays a longer game. Sam and Bobby bond over shared grief, sports, crushes on girls, and popular culture. Despite their differences, the boys' friendship is innately symbiotic and mutually beneficial with Sam teaching Roberto restraint, composure, and decency, while Roberto teaches Sam to come out of his shell a bit more and to cultivate his confidence. In that sense, each character spurs the other's primary character arc, with Sam helping Roberto to avoid the villainous trajectory that his anger has him on while Roberto empowers Sam's rise to prominence and, eventually, even a leadership role. Thus, their friendship isn't incidental to their respective characters, it's a defining attribute of who each of the characters is, woven directly into their respective journeys.

While Marvel editors may have been frustrated by Claremont's subversion of their intent for *The New Mutants*, the series sold well and earned a cult following, and the juxtaposition of innocent (for the most part) young characters and the horrors Claremont subjected them to actually enhanced a lot of the drama and tension by portraying the teens as constantly in over their head, a potent metaphor for adolescence in general. In this sense, Claremont's fears of expansion were—for the time being—unwarranted.

That changed, however, in 1986, when Claremont's concerns about losing creative control were realized as a group of Marvel creators and editors decided to resurrect Jean Grey to launch a new title featuring the original five X-Men called *X-Factor*. Claremont was incensed and very nearly quit: "Jim knew it would make money to bring her back. My counterargument was that the consequences to *X-Men* would be irreputable because the audience would never believe us. If we bring Jean back, there is no threat ever. If you bring Jean back then Scott has to abandon his wife and his new son and that's dishonorable. So you end up destroying Scott and what does that prove?" (personal interview 1). Unfortunately, Claremont and Shooter were both right. *X-Factor* sold well, but the creative impact was notable, and the X-Men franchise was now being written by more authors than just Christopher Claremont.

1988 saw the launch of two new titles and Claremont tackled them both this time—a task that required him to depart from his duties on *The New Mutants* after fifty-four issues. A *Wolverine* ongoing series and a British-based X-Men spin-off titled *Excalibur* both launched in the wake of that departure, both becoming long, ongoing titles of note. Claremont would only write nine of the first ten issues of the new *Wolverine* series, but he nonetheless laid a lot of groundwork in that time by taking the character into an adventure serial direction (analogous to the old *Terry and the Pirates* comic strip), while cultivating Logan's backstory with some unexpected twists and turns, emphasizing Wolverine's complex and enduring history and his advanced network of connections—and lingering enemies—accumulated through many years of hard living. At the same time, the genre shifts of the character from superhero (in *Uncanny X-Men*) to samurai (in the aforementioned *Wolverine* mini-series) to serial adventurer here helped establish a long-standing tradition of Wolverine as Marvel's most genre-diverse character, a malleable protagonist who can seemingly occupy the spotlight in whatever type of story a writer might wish to tell through him.

On the other side of the ocean, *Excalibur* was also something new for the X-Universe. Claremont's recipe started with the old

Captain Britain mythology. This was a mythology that Claremont himself had created years before for Marvel UK and was one that had been greatly cultivated through the work of later *Captain Britain* writers Jamie Delano and Alan Moore, alongside the inimitable pencil work of legendary comics artist Alan Davis. This *Captain Britain* mythology brought with it both the trappings of Arthurian romance and the delightful complexity of the Marvel multiverse, a concept created by Moore analogous to core concepts of the many worlds interpretation of quantum physics. Where other writers might have been tempted to wind back the *Captain Britain* mythology to what it was under their original stewardship, Claremont took the opposite approach: "I saw characters I'd created ages ago—such as Bri's twin sister, Betsy, and CID Commander Dai Thomas—totally changed, and all the better for it. I liked the people and I liked the book and my reaction at the end of each story was, what the heck comes next? And being a greedy, acquisitive sod, I couldn't wait for the chance to play with them myself" ("Introduction" 7).

Claremont combined this rich Captain Britain backstory with existing *X-Men* continuity and three *X-Men* characters who had been expelled from the series (for reasons discussed in the previous chapter) to form what seemed on the surface like the British wing of the X-Men. But where *X-Men* remained the staunchly serious text it had always been under Claremont, *Excalibur* drew from the theatrical genre of sex farce to create a sexually charged, character-based tragicomedy with deep explorations of relationships and characters. Where Claremont's *X-Men* was often acknowledged as having subversive representations of queer sexuality and a whole lot of kink (for lack of a better term), *Excalibur* put a spotlight on those elements, helping to normalize some of that subtext in a way that resonated with the series's core audience of the time. Speaking anecdotally, when interviewing Claremont, I suggested that *Excalibur* could be approached as "group therapy meets sex farce," and his immediate response was "I'd agree with that" (personal interview 2).

The series launches in a state of deep sorrow in the wake of tragedy. In "The Sword Is Drawn," Claremont brings together a team of superheroes all struggling (to various degrees) with suicidal ideation and depression. That a collective of such figures providing love and support to each other became a superhero team is a compelling angle. We see this mutual support in the face of suicidal ideation in a scene that finds Nightcrawler pushing himself beyond capacity to the point that Kitty questions whether Kurt is trying to join his fallen teammates through a course of suicidal recklessness. Kurt tells her that she has no right to say such things, to which Kitty responds, "You have no right to give me cause" (n.p.). Prior to this scene, we get another featuring Captain Britain (Brian Braddock) drinking himself to the point of stupor in a state of deep depression. When Meggan is unable to reach him, she asks herself, "Have I been fooling myself all these months, thinking you loved me? I couldn't bear that hurt. I'd rather be dead" (n.p.). Kurt, perhaps channeling Kitty's earlier admonishment, confronts Brian, pushing him against a wall and berating him in an attempt to spur him to rise to the challenge: "Mein Gott—sometimes all I yearn for, more than anything, is to have been given the chance, the privilege, of standing with the X-Men and sharing their fate! It isn't fair they're dead. It's far worse that I remain alive to grieve for them, because it's more pain than I can endure!!" (n.p.). Kurt ends his impassioned speech by stating, "But I am alive, Braddock! And I must remain true to myself, as to their memory." In doing so, Kurt presents his interior sense of duty (as Kitty did to Kurt) and calls on Brian (again somewhat virally) to do the same. These scenes (and others) of suicidal ideation play a key role in the foundations of the entire series and, particularly, in the relationships between the characters, who effectively form a support group that provides each other with assistance, community, and purpose. Taking that starting position to launch a book that is otherwise silly, raucous, and highly sexual creates a compelling stylistic juxtaposition capable of addressing and evoking a wide range of emotions.

The real secret weapon for Claremont on *Excalibur*, however, was penciller Alan Davis, a highly respected British artist who had done some fill-ins and annuals for the X-line. Davis's skill is hard to describe, but he is on record in an interview as taking a method approach to his figure drawing: "One of the things that I do with any group of characters that I work on is try to get under the skin of every character so that I become so familiar with him or her, that they actually exist in my head when I'm drawing them—so that I'm not drawing just stock figures" ("Introduction by Alan Davis from X-Men: Danger Room Battle Archives TPB (1996)" n.p.). This intuitive approach lends itself to a certain naturalness of figure, posture, and expression—one that is only possible with a preexisting mastery over structural method. The result is characters who speak volumes even when silent, even when standing in the background. Pairing this with Claremont's equally intuitive approach to character voice and consistency may be the key to *Excalibur*'s enduring appeal. It didn't hurt that Claremont and Davis were fans of each other as well, with Davis stating in a later interview, "I still regard him as the best writer I have ever collaborated with" ("Introduction by Alan Davis from X-Men: Danger Room Battle Archives TPB (1996)" n.p.).

As to the British backdrop of *Excalibur*, what we see is, essentially, a simulacrum of Britain more than a realistic depiction from Claremont, who left Britain at the age of three, and Davis, who lives in rural England and notes in an interview that "Excalibur is in London. I've only been to London on very few occasions. I hate the place" (qtd. in Zimmerman n.p.). Scholar, Nicholas Holm affirms this simulacrum aspect, arguing, "Claremont's Britain would seem to have its shallow foundations in cultural references, rather than a social existence, and therefore manifests almost entirely at the level of aesthetic surface" (n.p.). In short, then, the Britain of *Excalibur* is something of a fiction.

This is perhaps appropriate, however, as the most famous storyline produced by Claremont/Davis is "The Cross-Time Caper," which makes up a significant portion of the pair's *Excalibur* run

Figure 10. Excalibur reunites in "Moving Day" (*Excalibur*, vol. 1, no. 3). Alan Davis, penciller.

and takes place across a wild variety of alternate universes. Rather than being across "time," the caper is built around a tour of famous fictional universes, such as Thomas Mallory's *Le Morte D'Arthur*, T. H. White's *The Once and Future King*, Edgar Rice Burroughs's *John Carter of Mars*, Takachiho and Yasuhiko's *Dirty Pair*, Tatsuo Yoshida's *Speed Racer*, Wagner and Ezquerra's *Judge Dredd*, and is something analogous to *The Man in the High Castle* by Philip K. Dick. Interspersed or overlapped with these major arcs and storylines are brief touches to other fictional universes, such as those of *Doctor Who*, the *Lone Ranger*, and *Star Wars*. Thus, "The Cross-Time Caper" can be seen as something of a jam session, exploring and riffing on a series of iconic fictional universes in a fun and convivial manner.

In terms of character development and representation, one of the most remarkable portrayals in *Excalibur* is the toxic relationship between team members/romantic partners Captain Britain (Brian Braddock) and Meggan, which offers a rare and poignant portrayal of a dysfunctional coupling. Brian Braddock is a thirty-year-old man charged with being the magically enhanced protector of the British realm, a duty he despises. Meggan is an eighteen-year-old shapeshifter raised in isolation with television as her only source of companionship. So, there are some red flags here already for Meggan being largely incapable of a healthy relationship with an older man, and indeed Meggan's power set (as an empathic metamorph) serves as a metaphor—Meggan changes her body (often subconsciously) to match the desires of those around her. In this, she is quite literally adopting the toxic trait of defining herself through what her partner wants her to be, thus putting her in an even more vulnerable position.

Brian is not portrayed as simply a monstrous predator taking advantage of Meggan's vulnerability, however. Brian's behavior (which includes abandonment, casual infidelity, and even some emotional abuse) is portrayed sympathetically. Claremont, building on earlier work by Alan Moore in the pages of *Captain Britain*, portrays Brian as a broken person treating his trauma through a course of hedonistic and self-destructive behavior in the wake of an existential crisis. He is making unforgivable choices, but he's doing so in direct consequence of his depression and PTSD, and so instead of simply villain coding Brian as a soulless abuser, Claremont uses him to humanize the cycle of violence, to demonstrate how hurt people hurt people. In this, Claremont's work is again ahead of his time, arriving years before Paul Dini and Bruce Timm's "Mad Love" would win an Eisner Award for its depiction of similar themes in the Harley/Joker relationship with, arguably, a great deal less subtlety, particularly in the characterization of the abuser.

The final spin-off (if we want to call it that) to discuss is perhaps the most novel. At its core, *Classic X-Men* took the somewhat cynical practice of reprinting old *X-Men* comics and turned that crude bit of comics capitalism into something more innovative. The title launched in 1986 as a series featuring reprints of older *X-Men* issues, presented in order, beginning with *Giant-Size X-Men* #1, which was originally published ten years prior. This practice of reprinting old comics is very nearly as old as comics themselves and is especially familiar to the X-Men franchise, which existed only in the form of reprints from 1970 to 1975. But *Classic X-Men* had something else to offer: each reprinted issue came with a newly written story (as a sort of B-side) set in the original era of the reprint.

If this sounds confusing, it gets worse. Events depicted in the backup stories were then retroactively integrated into the ongoing *X-Men* continuity, such that a *Classic X-Men* backup story printed in 1988 but set in the *X-Men* continuity of 1978 could feature details that would then be considered canonical retroactively, as if they had always already occurred in the 1978 story. So, for example, if you were to read *X-Men Annual* #12 from 1988 ("Resurrection") and find yourself wondering why you don't recall when Storm met a transdimensional skyfox named C'Jime or when Colossus conceived a son with Nereel of the Fall People, you'd have to look for those answers in *Classic X-Men* #21 and #22, which chronicle both of these events as supplemental snippets to the new X-Men's first visit to the Savage Land, which was originally published (without skyfox or intimate encounter) way back in 1978.

This strategy of retroactive continuity additions is made more palatable due to the simple fact that the writer from 1978 is the same in 1988, but even so this approach to continuity is somewhat experimental and compelling to study for its own sake, even without the otherwise unpublished important moments that became the subject of these stories. These include Magneto's origin story, the forming of the Starjammers, the exact nature of the Phoenix Force's offering to Jean, Mastermind's slow seduction of Jean, the sexual threat that Logan presented to Jean's relationship, and many more deeply important moments in X-Men continuity.

But the contributions to X-Men continuity are about much more than plot details. The *Classic X-Men* stories emphasized intimate character portraits over the usual group action dynamic of *Uncanny X-Men*. Claremont notes, "They quickly became surprisingly and intensely personal ones for me as a writer. I was getting into the characters' heads and souls with a focus that often wasn't available in the regular book and doing so with a perspective of better than a decade's worth of work on the title" ("Introduction to X-Men: Vignettes" n.p.). With space to breathe and hindsight to guide his perspective, Claremont would often isolate one or two X-Men characters and build a narrative that provided key insight to the depth of their character, even retrospectively.

This emphasis on character is ably met by a more intimate artistic style provided by artist John Bolton (the man that Claremont teamed with on *Marada the She-Wolf* and *Black Dragon* as well): "With him I could tell stories that simply wouldn't fit in the fast-paced, widescreen, mega-action adventure ensemble of the main series itself. I could take a slower pace. I could focus. I could stretch some boundaries (even if they were only internal) and maybe break some rules. And have some serious fun in the process" ("Introduction to X-Men: Vignettes" n.p.). Bolton's distinctive artwork moves away from the house style of Marvel at the time, invoking instead a hyperrealist, photographic style that gives the characters a sense of presence and realization that added a visual depth to each character to match the narrative depth of Claremont's vignettes.

Outside of Bolton's contributions to the *Classic X-Men* aesthetic, the series also boasts some remarkable cover artwork, including twenty-two covers by Art Adams, twenty-two by Steve Lightle, and fourteen by a pre-*Hellboy* Mike Mignola, with each artist providing a unique essentialization of iconic X-Men stories and moments, informed once again by the value and perspective of hindsight.

Comic book reprints are, by tradition, worth just about as much as the paper that they're printed on, except in very rare circumstances. But the backup stories in *Classic X-Men* offer readers a uniquely anachronistic experience in retroactive continuity, enabled and empowered by Claremont's long tenure on the X-Men franchise. The publisher's motivation is perhaps cynical, and the chronology certainly confusing, but *Classic X-Men* was a unique and important moment in the history of this franchise and, when we consider how wholly unlikely the circumstances empowering it were, maybe in the history of the comics medium as well.

All told, with each of these spin-offs Claremont demonstrated both the enduring capacity for the X-Men universe to expand and adapt and his own capacity as a writer to tell different kinds of stories in different ways. These spin-offs were more than proofs of a concept, however. In their own way, each represents a beloved, enduring, and accomplished title, providing the world of comics with memorable characters and concepts and moments.

CHAPTER FIVE

Two Infernos

The Silvestri and Lee Years and the Departure

> These, to me, sadly, are living characters. They have always been people. The frustration on my end is why do I seem to be among the few people who comprehend that?
> —Chris Claremont (personal interview 2)

It took a long time for the aftermath of the paradigm shift that was "The Mutant Massacre" for *X-Men* to settle into a new status quo but, when it did, Claremont's mutants had a new home, a revised roster, and a new penciller. Within this altered paradigm, Claremont pushed toward the most ambitious story of his entire career, "Inferno," before new voices entered the picture and the Claremont run on *X-Men* came to an abrupt end.

This era is identified by Jason Powell as Claremont's "most radical departure from the traditional X-Men status quo. Virtually all of the franchise's recognizable signifiers are gone." At the same time, however, the creative experimentation pays off for Powell, who calls this "one of the most creatively rich eras of Claremont's tenure" (185). The Outback era, as it's called in honor of the team taking residence in the Australian Outback, is often singled out by fans as an all-time favorite in X-Men continuity, despite the absence of iconic X-Men characters such as Cyclops, Kitty Pryde, Professor X, and Nightcrawler.

The team's tenure in the Outback was far briefer than many fans might assume. The team assaults the villainous Reavers and occupy their Outback base in UXM #229 ("Down Under"), published May 1988, and they would abandon the base to those same Reavers in issue #251 ("Fever Dream") from July 1989, just fourteen months later. And while the Outback setting was the X-Men's base for the aforementioned "Inferno" storyline, most of that story takes place away from the Outback, in New York City. Thus, identifying why fans latch onto this era so frequently is a bit of a challenge, with many options available. This was an era of existential dread for the team, of rising tension, and, for Claremont, of creative exploration beyond anything he had previously attempted.

Claremont's copilot in this era was a young penciller named Marc Silvestri. Silvestri was a mainstay for X-Men, contributing to fifty-six issues of UXM during the Claremont run, both before and after the Outback era, though it's the during part that would seem to have achieved the most enduring resonance. On UXM, Silvestri was paired with Dan Green, who had joined the series as a regular inker way back in issue #179, thus providing some continuity for the series across disparate art styles in the pencils. Silvestri notes at this time, "I can't stress enough how happy I am to be working with Dan Green as an inker. To a penciller, a good inker is more valuable than gold. Dan, I think, is one of the best in the business" (qtd. in Hembeck n.p.).

Silvestri holds artist Frank Frazetta as a great influence. As such, the Frazetta style is all over Silvestri's portion of the run, advancing the key themes of the era in significant ways. Frazetta is well known for violent, kinetic action, compelling monsters, and hypermasculinity with accompanying sexualization of female characters, and, true to influence, all these elements show up in abundance during the Outback era. Frazetta is further known for specifically defining the aesthetic of a genre called "sword and sandals" (think Conan, a character Frazetta drew quite often). This aesthetic carried over in the work of Silvestri, placing emphasis on the harshness of nature/existence and sweaty, gritty heroes. This gave readers an X-Men team that were visibly worn down, overtaxed, and isolated, a sharp departure from the usual mansion-dwelling

Figure 11. Wolverine takes action in the Outback in "Down Under" (*Uncanny X-Men*, vol. 1, no. 229). Marc Silvestri, penciller.

superheroes they'd been for most of their existence beforehand. This visual texture that Silvestri brought to life in *X-Men* not only sells their depletion from the past (before the "Fall of the Mutants" storyline) but also propels the narrative toward the "Inferno" event by visually capturing the isolation and spiritual exhaustion that ultimately makes the X-Men vulnerable to the demonic forces who incite the inferno in Claremont's longest percolating story arc.[1]

Ahead of "Inferno," Claremont's Outback team fought cyborg raiders in the spirit of Mad Max, a return of the alien Brood in the spirit of a *Twilight Zone* episode (complete with a fallible narrator who doesn't know he's possessed by a malevolent alien), and white-collar mutant enslavers in a brilliant little allegory for apartheid South Africa that Jason Powell describes as "Claremont's all-time best for Uncanny X-Men, applying its analogies deftly and carefully—and keeping them implicit throughout" (194). And then, "Inferno" begins, unfolding across the pages of *Uncanny X-Men*, *X-Factor*, and *New Mutants* (the three core X-books of the time) but also spilling over into innumerable other Marvel properties, including *Fantastic Four, Daredevil, Spider-Man*, and *the Avengers*. The core story is that a member of the New Mutants, Illyana Rasputin, is tricked into raising hell on earth and the current roster of X-Men, combined with X-Factor, must put it right by battling the villainous Mister Sinister and a whole lot of demons in what's left of New York City. Their main foe, however, is one of their own—Madelyne Pryor, the longtime X-Men ally who also happens to be Cyclops's estranged/abandoned wife and mother to his son (who will grow up to be the very popular character Cable). Madelyne is also the current lover of Cyclops's brother Havok at this point. Madelyne, motivated by maternal instinct combined with a mounting sense of frustration and hurt, has made a deal with the devil, so to speak, to find her lost son. As with all such deals, the cost will be her soul, and we as readers are left to watch the demons come to collect when Madelyne transforms from a beloved heroine to "the Goblin Queen" of a new hellscape.

The depth of character development in the series in the buildup to "Inferno" is notable. Greatly enhancing the story here is the culmination of years upon years of character development at a depth and level that exceeds even "The Dark Phoenix Saga." As rich as the characters were in that storyline, a decade later they have grown and changed considerably; their voices have become more distinct, just as new voices have been added to the cast, each with something new to offer. Claremont's characters were strong to begin with, but in exploring the canvas provided by years of storytelling in the X-Men universe, time made them better. "Inferno" gives us a Wolverine who is both noble and primal; a Cyclops who is both duty bound and selfish; an Archangel who is both brutal and idealistic; and a Storm who is both merciful and not at all someone to be messed with. Their voices are distinct and honed and their characters can encompass the complexity of competing dualities. If, as I have argued, Claremont's greatest strength as a writer is in-depth characterization and cultivating obscenely long continuous narratives, then, by those terms, "Inferno" is his magnum opus, exploring both to a degree so far removed from Stan Lee's famous adage that "every comic is somebody's first" as to make the story virtually inaccessible to a modern audience. Simply put, this is Claremont at his utmost and the result is a deeply engaging story that stands out among Claremont's best.

And still Claremont continues to push the status quo in the wake of "Inferno," first with a pair of comical and satiric issues oriented on gender rituals ("Ladies Night" and "Men"); then with the catastrophic unraveling of the team, with Rogue falling in battle to the mutant-hunting robot Mastermold; and then, just an issue later, with Longshot leaving the team to find himself and Storm seemingly killed by Havok in a friendly fire incident, leaving the team without a leader. With Wolverine AWOL, the Outback team is left to stand with just four members: Dazzler, Colossus, Havok, and Psylocke, none of whom are emotionally capable of carrying forward Xavier's dream. After just one mission, they too fall apart, and Claremont does the unthinkable: effectively disbanding the team in the most dramatic fashion possible. The era that follows is sometimes referred to as the "Dissolution and Rebirth" era, a name used in Marvel's "Epic Collection" anthology reprint. Powell describes this era as "Claremont's 'Russian Novel' phase, in which Claremont has not only disassembled the current roster, but he's abandoned the entire concept of the X-Men as a 'team' at all" (235). The story it tells is bizarre, focusing on a cosmic realignment of the lives of Dazzler, Psylocke, Colossus, Rogue, and Havok, who are mystically gifted with new identities that each serve as a sort of cipher of their innermost character. This plot device provides Claremont with a narrative tool by which to telegraph characters' interior desires.

Colossus gets to be a Soho artist. It speaks to his gentle, creative soul and the tragedy created by his mutant powers, due to the responsibility that goes with them, taking him away from the artist's life. Psylocke becomes an emotionless assassin with a physicality and outward demeanor that more closely reflects the warrior heart and attitude that she expresses in earlier issues. Rogue is dropped right back in her room in the Outback base, solidifying the notion that being an X-Man is in fact her personal paradise (which is consistent for her redemption arc discussed in a previous chapter). Dazzler goes back to the life of fame she once aspired to. She gets to sing and act and be fawned on by everyone, allowing her to move past some of her haunting personal anxieties. Havok gets to be a government magistrate/soldier. In the wake of several tragedies, Havok was plagued by anger and a longing for structure, purpose, and authorization to use his power in ways that a superhero can't. All of them, of course, end up right back on the X-Men eventually. These character vignettes are structured around two distinct parties slowly but surely gathering the X-Men back together, with the whole dissolution and rebirth storyline spanning an impressive twenty-two issues of the series, which, again, is titled *Uncanny X-Men* at a time when that team doesn't exist. The two parties working toward reunification are Forge/Banshee and Wolverine/Jubilee (and eventually Psylocke).

Claremont's pairing of Banshee and Forge has them serving as torchbearers of the X-Men's legacy, and the hope of reunification offers some intriguing contrasts and juxtapositions that make the unlikely duo oddly effective at bridging generations of X-Men teams. They have an obvious May–December relationship going with Banshee, a character cultivated in the silver age of comics, representing a long-standing history, and Forge, a character only recently cultivated, representing an emerging new guard. We can see this role for Banshee in things like his connections to Irish mythology (leprechauns and keeps and a shillelagh-wielding cousin), alongside the dubious silver age physics of his superpowers in which he flies by screaming. On Forge's side, we see the future of comics: big technology (including cyborg parts), big guns, gritty backstory, and a morally compromised hero in over his head amid competing forces of ambiguous ethical standards. Forge brings drive and motivation; Banshee brings experience and credibility. Together, they encompass the X-Men past and the X-Men future, working together to draw back the X-Men of the present. It's a fun dynamic that ably transitions the book into a new era.

On the other side of the narrative (and sometimes the planet), the Jubilee/Wolverine relationship is colored by a quiet desperation on the part of Jubilee (Jubilation Lee), the American-born teen whose Chinese immigrant parents are recently deceased. Jubilee quickly latches onto Wolverine as a substitute parent, but that relationship is tense, constantly threatened by Logan's diminishing health and his apparent death wish at this point in the series. In keeping with Claremont's interest in contrasting character exterior behavior with interior desire, Jubilee is outwardly bombastic, confrontational, and enthusiastic, but this belies an interior existence that is often revealed to be frightened and lonely. The pair form a codependent duo, first keeping each other alive and then giving each other a reason to live. This is especially important for Logan, whose story has been leading the character toward self-destruction, and, with the X-Men gone, that threat is even larger. Jubilee quickly becomes fiercely loyal to Wolverine, showing a deep sensitivity to his well-being and a fierce defensiveness against anyone who might threaten him, or even anyone who might usurp her position as Logan's friend and confidante. In all of this, the Jubilee/Logan relationship adds a sort of specificity to the found family metaphor that is the centerpiece of *X-Men* comics. They need each other at a desperate level, and both are simply holding on for dear life while trying to scrounge together what's left of the X-Men.

Toward the end of the dissolution era, Claremont introduces the final new X-Man of his tenure. When Gambit is first introduced, it is as a foil character to Storm (who herself has a new life/identity at this point). Gambit, a thief and scoundrel, offers Storm the path not taken, tempting her with an existence that is the opposite of the responsibilities she shoulders as leader of the X-Men. Where it appears that Gambit is corrupting Storm, the opposite slowly becomes evident. Storm isn't lured over to Gambit's life; Gambit is lured over to hers. What starts as an intense curiosity about the legendary "Storm" becomes a deep admiration for Storm's willpower, leadership, and heroism. Through his association with her, Gambit becomes a hero, demonstrating again the viral nature of Xavier's dream. At the same time, Claremont offers Storm an alternative life to live at an integral moment in her character arc. Thanks to the villain Nanny, Storm is given an entirely new life and thus she can unburden herself of the X-Men if that's what she really wants. Storm rejects this opportunity to return to the X-Men, however, and, through Gambit, Claremont shows us again who, by her choice, Storm truly is.

The final ongoing penciller to pair with Claremont in the pages of *X-Men* was Jim Lee, a man whose impact on comics as both an artist and a businessman would reshape the industry in the 1990s. Building on inspiration from previous *X-Men* illustrator John Byrne, Jim Lee cultivated and popularized a new application of cinematic style to the X-Men universe, one that specifically drew on the newest wave of cinematic aesthetic. The results were visually striking, producing the kind of awed responses that Byrne

Figure 12. Jim Lee and Scott Williams for "The Key That Breaks the Locke" (*Uncanny X-Men*, vol. 1, no. 256). Jim Lee, penciller.

himself was generating with a cinematic style inspired by a 1970s film vocabulary. This contrasts with Lee's work, which shows more resemblance to the so-called MTV Generation of TV/film with low angles, frenetic action, and a heavy emphasis on style. Helping Lee achieve this aesthetic was inker Scott Williams, with whom Lee formed a career-long partnership. The pair quickly developed a deep sense of synergy. "There was a lot of things that he would put in the pencils, which weren't really native to his style, but sort of fit the type of line and the type of look that I was looking for" (Avila n.p.). As the X-Men slowly reformed within Claremont's narrative,[2] the Lee/Williams aesthetic created a sense of renewal and rejuvenation, a palpable excitement for the series that belied the simmering creative tensions underneath.

And then the unthinkable happened. At the time of Claremont's departure from Marvel Comics, he was the best-selling comics writer in the industry, a career company man who had been staunchly loyal to Marvel Comics for decades. That they would want to get rid of him is therefore unusual, but the historical record depicts a conflict of wills and egos and, above all else, choices. Austin Gorton of the Real Gentlemen of Leisure website describes the situation from the perspective of Claremont's fans:

> Much has been written about Claremont's departure, how it was handled, who was to blame. He received a raw deal, no doubt about it, pushed aside in favor of the hot new thing (which, in a delightful bit of schadenfreude, shortly thereafter pushed aside the people who booted Claremont), despite his decades of history and the level of his success, elevating an afterthought of a title into an industry juggernaut. His departure, while necessary in the eyes of the powers-that-be, was handled poorly and by most accounts, unprofessionally. (n.p.)

This charge of poor professionalism was lobbed very directly by Claremont at his editor, Bob Harras. In an interview, Harras provides the account of his perspective on the situation:

> I felt like we had to go back to what *X-Men* was all about, and to me *X-Men* was Xavier and Scott and Jean and all the other classic characters. But Chris didn't want to do that kind of stuff any more. He felt that he had done it already. My point was, "Sure, *that's* the X-Men!" It was getting so we were speaking the same language, but we couldn't understand each other. Also, at that point, I was getting whispers from the sales department, saying that the retailers were unhappy. There was a subtle pressure from that direction to do something drastic with the book. It was doing well enough, but I got these rumblings that excitement wasn't there any more. It had the numbers still, that was Chris' point, and it was valid. His books had the best sales by far in the industry. He had made it the number one book. Why mess with that? But, on the other hand, I knew I had a great asset in Jim [Lee], who also had feelings about the direction he wanted the stories to take. It was like, "Which way do we go?" (qtd. in DeFalco 178)

Harras's inclination leaned toward Jim Lee, who was already in the habit of faxing directions for the need to "pump up" Claremont's plots, something Claremont resented. In a letter dated April 4, 1991, Claremont took his complaint to Marvel vice president Michael Hobson, asking:

> Am I a creative artist in my own right, or merely a pair of hands transcribing another person's vision? . . . Two years ago, Louise Simonson and I accounted between us for forty percent of Marvel's direct sales. I would wager that percentage held true last year as well. . . . Yet she has gone, in anger and bitterness, and I feel that I'm a small step away from being booted after her. . . . To be honest, this is a letter I never conceived of writing. A situation I never thought would have to be addressed. I find myself looking at the body of work that encompasses nearly half my life, that I am very proud of, and wondering why I bothered. I look at a company that I have loyally served for longer than most of the people currently working there, and again wonder why I bothered. (Papers)

From there, correspondence between Claremont and Harras continued to get more contentious, with Harras noting, "None of this is meant to be taken as an insult or punishment, Chris" while informing Claremont that his stories were being altered (Papers). Claremont responds:

> I am in receipt of your fax of 9 april, and appreciate your frankness. I further appreciate the fact that, although you were given full plots for both the issues involved . . . you made not the slightest effort to work with me as the writer on the book to bring them to a point where they would prove acceptable to you. But chose instead to hand them over to Jim and Whilce [Portacio] to handle any and all required modifications. (Papers)

By April 23, Claremont again petitioned Michael Hobson to intervene, observing:

> The plain fact of the matter is that my editor has intentionally and deliberately acted to defraud me. . . . This is not the basis for any sort of positive working relationship. Indeed, in mainstream prose publishing houses—and this I know from personal experience—it is grounds for immediate dismissal for the employee/editor responsible. . . . This is intolerable. If something is not done to set things right, and done quickly, then I see no hopes whatsoever for a positive resolution. (Papers)

Harras's resolution was to give the reins to Jim Lee while offering Claremont the opportunity to continue scripting the series. Lee would provide the plots, the core of the narrative storytelling. Claremont would fill in the dialogue. Claremont was wounded and insulted by this arrangement but nonetheless acquiesced to fill in the text and thought bubbles of someone else's stories with the characters he had cultivated. Eventually, however, the situation proved untenable. Claremont departed, negotiating to write one final story arc as his severance package, the first issue of which would go on to become the best-selling single-issue comic of all time, a record that stands today.

In hindsight, Claremont describes this time in his life as such:

> There was just all this butting of heads and we all got boxed into corners. Bob and Jim wanted to do what they wanted to do and the feeling was I could not or would not go along, and they were going to do it anyway. I thought, I've worked too hard. The time has come maybe to see if I can survive without the X-Men. So I quit *X-Men* and left Marvel. (qtd. in DeFalco 75–76)

And that was the end of the Claremont run, the longest, and possibly finest (in the eyes of devotees), single-author run in the history of Marvel Comics. Eventually the drama and clash of personalities that readers knew from the books had found their way into the life of the author himself. And just like that, it was all over.

Decades later, Claremont's hindsight on the mercantile nature of storytelling within the Marvel Universe offers readers a somewhat bleak picture of a man who loved his characters more than his chosen industry could possibly support:

> As Stan [Lee] beat in my head 50 years ago: these aren't my toys. These are Marvel's toys. Every time you get them you get to play with them for a while and then put them back on the shelf, where they belong. Then the next writer comes along and takes them off the shelf and does all sorts of cool stuff from their perspective. If you want to change things, irrevocably, that's a big deal. But, sadly, it's also an irrelevant deal, because someone will come along down the line, and put them back the way they were. And the readers are left with the conundrum of "who do I believe?" The characters who they were? The characters who they are? Or the characters they will become? It gets very complicated. ("I'm Chris Claremont" n.p.)

These questions need not be rhetorical, however. The shadow that Claremont's sixteen-year run of X-Men storytelling casts continues to shape the franchise decades later, with key characters, storylines, and crossover titles from this era continuing to surface in the works of modern creators. And though Claremont was never able to achieve the unique alchemy that defined this run (his most renowned era of comics storytelling), he wasn't altogether finished telling *X-Men* stories, and he certainly wasn't done telling stories in general.

CHAPTER SIX

Returning Legend

Subsequent Returns and Other Notable Works

> I'm not dead yet.
> —Chris Claremont (personal interview 2)

Claremont went in a lot of directions upon leaving Marvel Comics. He wrote novels in the Lucasfilm Willow franchise as well as novelizations of two of the 20th Century Fox X-Men films. He cultivated a project called "The Huntsman" for the fledgling Image Comics that failed to launch. He returned to Marvel in a role that gave him some administrative oversight and creative influence. He went to DC and got to write iconic characters such as Superman, Batman, and Wonder Woman. He wrote in the Predator vs. Aliens franchise. He created characters in *Big Hero 6* (Fredzilla and Wasabi) that would be featured in a Disney film of the same name. He even got to return to his original run on X-Men in an alternate universe continuation series called *X-Men Forever* and also got to write an alternate universe ending for the X-Men franchise in *X-Men: The End*.

To date, however, the author has never achieved the same level of success that he did with his run on X-Men. Douglas Wolk argues, "As the *X-Men* went adrift without Claremont, he did the same without them" (165). Jason Powell takes a similar perspective while adding a positive spin in that "Claremont's accomplishment on *X-Men* from 1975–1991 simply cannot be duplicated, not even by him. This is not necessarily a bad thing. His output during that time was singular and special, and should be treasured for the brilliant, one-of-a-kind work of art that it is" (275). His later career is still notable. His work is good, maybe even important. But it didn't make the same impact. Nonetheless, there's a lot here to appreciate, and painting a broader picture of the life of Claremont's work and influence demands the enterprise.

When Whilce Portacio was unable to pair with Claremont on his proposed 1992 "The Huntsman" project for Image Comics, Claremont decided instead to join Marvel's longest competitor, DC, with an original series called *Sovereign Seven* that Wolk describes as "an X-Men coffee shop AU" (166). Though it lasted only thirty-six issues, *Sovereign Seven* holds a unique place in the history of DC comics, as Brian Cronin notes:

> What made the book unique is that it was a creator-owned series, but it was set firmly inside the confines of the DC Universe. It is an arrangement that neither DC nor Marvel had ever made with any other comic book creators, but as the first new superhero series by Claremont after leaving Uncanny X-Men following a nearly 17-year run making the X-Men the most popular comic book series in the entire industry, it was a bet that DC was willing to make. (n.p.)

The series's debut in May 1995 was successful, thanks to the much-heralded return of Chris Claremont to comics. As Cronin notes, it was the only DC comic to crack the Top 10 that month. The series failed to latch onto a committed following, however, and fell out of the top 100 within the same year (Cronin n.p.). Creatively, the series had a lot in common with Claremont's earlier work, focusing as it did on a found family of superheroes with the same internal conflicts and slow-burning mysteries that characterized his X-Men years. It also drew upon themes of mind control and alternate evil selves who signal their villainy through signifiers of BDSM in their revised costumes. The second issue of the series even features a sneaky cameo by Wolverine that is off panel, but clearly indicated (figure 13). None of this could help it overcome

Figure 13. Wolverine in "Sovereign Seven" (*Sovereign Seven*, vol. 1, no. 2). Dwayne Turner, penciller.

its sales deficiencies, however, and the series was canceled after three years.

Shortly thereafter, Claremont began another much-heralded assignment, an improbable return to Marvel Comics initiated by Bob Harras himself. Alec Foege describes the sequence of events leading up to this as follows:

> Harras realized he needed help—Marvel's sales were declining, and the comics were getting harder to follow. He and Claremont hadn't spoken in five years. Then in 1995, at the annual August comics convention in San Diego, Harras spotted Claremont at an outdoor buffet. Partly because a friend bet him $5 that he wouldn't have the nerve, Harras went up to him at a picnic table. Suddenly, the whole place fell silent. "It was like one of those old E. F. Hutton commercials," recalls Harras. Two years later, Claremont returned to Marvel as Harras's No. 2, with the title of vice president/editorial director. (n.p.)

This led Claremont, eventually, to the job of writing *The Fantastic Four* in 1998. Claremont's affection for the FF (and Ben Grimm, a.k.a. the Thing, in particular) is something that was readily visible anytime Claremont had the opportunity to write the characters in his previous Marvel stint.[1] The FF was also a franchise that lent itself well to the science-fiction genre, a favorite of Claremont, who was both well read in the genre and well networked with an entire generation of science-fiction writers.

Claremont's storytelling with *The Fantastic Four* was ambitious here again and wildly convoluted with alternate realities colliding in a manner that is quite similar to *X-Men*'s "Days of Future Past" storyline but more focused on exploring the concept of the villain/hero relationship, particularly with Reed Richards having a brief stint in the role of Dr. Doom. Claremont's *FF* run was short again (just twenty-nine issues), but his storytelling was ambitious, and the run has something of a cult following; as Bill Kte'pi of *How to Love Comics* notes, "His FF is a deep cut, a neglected curiosity" (n.p.).

Eventually—perhaps inevitably—Claremont found his way back to *X-Men*. Sean Howe quotes an anonymous editor, stating, "Technically, Chris was not supposed to be involved in the X-Men, but there was no way to keep them away from him" (403). Thus, May 2000 saw the launch of the "Revolution" event in *X-Men*, in which Claremont teamed with a new generation of artists in order to recapture the magic of previous years and to reposition the franchise as the tentpole property that Marvel needed it to be, but it came at a time when Marvel was in a dire financial situation and facing pressures that were not conducive to creative success. The situation is summarized by Dirk Deppey of *The Comics Journal*:

> Jemas and Quesada wasted no time in transforming Marvel's publishing philosophy from a conservative, formulaic reliance on established superhero tropes to a more adventurous, whatever-sticks-to-the-walls approach, conducted in the shadow of ironclad market reality. Both men made clear in interviews that they clearly understood that growth in Marvel's publishing division meant walking a fine line between two seemingly incompatible constituencies—on the one hand, the company needed to maintain its existing base, while on the other, it also needed to experiment with new genres and storytelling techniques, in order to appeal to potential readers who might not be interested in what the existing fanbase craved. (qtd. in Darowski 120)

This duality was especially problematic for the X-Men franchise, with a blockbuster movie release in 2000 fostering hope that cinemagoers would follow their favorite new superheroes to the comics they had originated from.

While Claremont would again revisit a lot of key story beats from his previous run on *X-Men,* he also showed a commitment to evolving the characters beyond the status quo, often within a linear trajectory from his original *X-Men* run. A good example of this transpires in issue #103 of *X-Men,* when Rogue fights Wolverine one-on-one to decide leadership of the X-Men in a story that harkens back to Claremont's first run on *UXM* and to his cultivation of Rogue's character arc—one of the longest and most satisfying face turns in comics history. The story is an obvious homage to Cyclops and Storm dueling for leadership of the team in *Uncanny X-Men* #201 ("Duel"), discussed in a previous chapter. In that same original run, Claremont portrayed Rogue as a truly reluctant hero—a villain who joined the team but by no means a repentant villain. Rogue is there for the mental health benefits package of being an X-Man: the help of Charles Xavier. It would take years for Rogue to truly develop her heroic tendencies in a densely layered character arc that unfolds so gradually that even Rogue herself fails to grasp just how virtuous and righteous she's become. She finds herself slowly but surely, even to the point of martyrdom during the original Claremont run. In *X-Men* #103 ("The Goth"), new team member, Tessa, provides the best assessment of this remarkable evolution by telling Rogue, "Here you are, among those who were once your bitter enemies, and you are welcome. You have made a place for yourself and proved your worth" (3). Once known for being hotheaded, irresponsible, and petulant, Rogue is unanimously acclaimed as a leader, with Wolverine (after losing to her superior intelligence in their duel) telling her to "take the job you've earned. You lead" (14). Rogue's arrival as leader of the team is a welcome moment in the series—a natural and compelling extension of the decade-long character arc that Claremont had built around her slow and painful journey of atonement.

In "Revolution," Claremont also shows a renewed commitment to diversity in representation by recentring women of color Cecilia Reyes and Charlotte Jones into the narrative from the outset, launching another woman of color in Karima Shapandar, and introducing Neal Sharra as the newest team member and the first Indian X-Man in comics history. Neal Sharra thus holds a lot of potential to reach an untapped audience and to increase the representational profile of the X-Men franchise, a profile near and dear to Claremont's heart. Unfortunately, Thunderbird III (as he was code named) never had that impact and the character has been virtually abandoned ever since. As noted by scholar Joe Darowski, "Although India has a very diverse set of ethnicities and cultural groups, we are not told much about the character's heritage other than that he is Indian and his family lives in Calcutta" (113). Darowski further notes that Neal's powers are "almost identical to Sunfire," while I would add that there's a lot of similarities to Havok in terms of Neal's vexed relationship to his own powers. In short, the character didn't stand out in a lot of ways, and his ethnicity was underconsidered.

In order to bring visual life to Claremont's X-Men return, Marvel teamed the fifty-year-old writer with twenty-three-year-old penciller Lenil Francis Yu. Though both creators would achieve creative heights in the pages of *X-Men*, they, arguably, did not do so together. Yu, though aesthetically gifted, is quite evidently a masterful visual storyteller when given space to do so, something he would prove with his work on *Superman: Birthright* and something he would continue to prove, even up to his more recent work on *X-Men* comics without Chris Claremont. Claremont's text-heavy style (firmly out of fashion in a postimage era) may not have paired well with Yu's ability to work with the page (rather than the panel) as the main unit of composition. Without space to operate, Yu's work comes off a little flat compared to later efforts.

The centerpiece of Claremont's first issue of "Revolution" is a revamped Kitty Pryde, with the author cultivating a more mature incarnation of his character, but there's some inconsistencies in

Figure 14. The new Kitty Pryde in "End of Days" (*X-Men*, vol. 2, no. 100). Lenil Francis Yu, penciller.

the portrayal and some potentially problematic issues in the handling of Kitty's sexuality. This idea of character progression is compelling, especially for a character who can easily get lumped into a state of perpetual adolescence in the eyes of the readership, something that Claremont might be commenting on directly in Kitty's dialogue in X-Men #100 ("End of Days"): "What do you want from me, Peter? To be the girl I was when we first met? Reboot your system, baby, 'cause time only goes in one direction. You all have this vision of sweet little Kitty . . . that you want to freeze in amber. . . . I walk through walls—between rooms and between worlds!" (21). Nonetheless there are issues that undermine this evolution. For one thing, it ignores the preexisting continuity of Kitty Pryde as a character. Kitty was already (somewhat artificially) aged up during Warren Ellis's late 1990s run on *Excalibur*. Additionally, some of the imagery surrounding Kitty might seem to be catering to the male gaze, and a lot of the scenes themselves put Kitty in vulnerable positions.

As an aside, in a different story from 2002's *X-Men Unlimited* #36 ("This One's for You!"), however, Claremont again takes a modern look at Kitty Pryde but here defines her maturity through her emotional growth and pain. Kitty's character growth is quite evident in a story that compares being an X-Man to being a war veteran. Where Claremont and Byrne initially defined Kitty through boundless optimism and energy, *X-Men Unlimited* #36 gives us a Kitty who has lost that in consequence of successive exposure to tragedy, death, and hatred—highlighted by the fact that she's left superheroism behind to go to college. This depiction is consistent with Claremont's initial approach to *X-Men*, his desire to age the characters in real time, alter them over the course of events, and renew the team constantly as characters quit. The story opens with key scenes from Kitty's *UXM* days, skillfully illustrated by Salvador Larroca but with narrative captions that recontextualize these prior events as tragic (in hindsight) and Kitty as naïve for her earlier enthusiasm: "I got my wish. I became one of the X-Men. I helped save the world. I helped save the universe! I went to the stars. Best of all, I fell in love. But no matter what I did, people refused to see us for who we truly were. All that mattered was the label. Mutant. Outcast. Enemy" (4). Kitty builds a new life for herself along the path not taken originally when she decided to join the X-Men. Unable to acclimate to this new world, she distances herself and obsesses over the past, particularly on the death of her father. She is spurred, however, to heroism twice: first in rescuing someone else's father from a burning building and second by violently defeating antimutant radicals on her campus. In both instances, we see the heroic impulse (and the old Kitty) surfacing. The story ends with Kitty promising to make her father proud but not really sure which direction that will take her as either a superhero or a scholar. It's a sweet, melancholy moment, which offers the character yet another life-defining choice.

Claremont's return run on *X-Men* led directly into a new title, *X-Treme X-Men* (2001–2004), which also featured some good comics storytelling and the occasional glimpse of the strong character work that defined Claremont's first run on *Uncanny X-Men*. Claremont returned again to the franchise in 2004, an even briefer run that is perhaps highlighted by the "End of Greys" storyline (*Uncanny X-Men* #466–71), which sees Claremont cultivate the Rachel Summers character further by subjecting her to even more unthinkable tragedy. By 2006, Claremont had finished his last run on *Uncanny X-Men* comics to date. Soon after, however, he began writing alternate universe X-Men stories that allowed him creative control of his original X-Men storylines through tales that were noncanonical to the mainline Marvel Universe. This also allowed Claremont to abandon canon established by the X-writers who'd followed his first run on *X-Men*. A simple example would be Claremont's choice to return the franchise to its original plan of making Sabretooth Wolverine's father.

Though he may not have found a defining title to call home, Claremont continued writing throughout the 2010s, closing out the decade with another return to his earlier work in 2019's *New Mutants: War Children*, which is set between issues of Claremont's original *New Mutants* run and shows a deft touch in recapturing the voices of the characters that he created, despite the gap of years and the many different permutations of the characters that we've seen since. The story reunites Claremont with Bill Sienkiewicz, who remains at the top of his game with vivid, surrealist renderings. Importantly, though, the story starts with a bang, flashes through a series of familiar conflicts, and ends with a mess to clean up. In

Figure 15. Art from "War Children" (*New Mutants: War Children*, vol. 1, no. 1). Bill Sienkiewicz, penciller.

its role as a love letter to the original run, it works—pulling on the nostalgia strings by giving readers one more impossible moment with a team they loved.

And indeed, the author's claim that he's not dead yet merits respect. Even just in interviewing the man, it is clear to me that Claremont is and forever will be a storyteller. It is clear as well to the thousands of fans who line up to speak with him and get his autograph at the innumerable conventions that Claremont still travels to, despite being a man in his seventies. Most who encounter him will tell of an author who is more likely to "talk your ear off" than to rush you through the line.

Who knows what he might have put to pen in the time since this book is published? And if the answer in the mind of the reader is "nothing of note," that's fine too. Most authors (Shakespeare, Austen, Wells) have a golden period of roughly five years in which their greatest works come to the surface. Different fans and scholars will always argue when exactly the golden age of Claremont was (I'm partial to 1988–1991 myself), but that too speaks to range and accomplishment. For sixteen years, Chris Claremont wrote something special, and while the returns might have diminished a bit in the years that followed that first run, there were still returns, still ideas and innovations, still stories worth telling.

CONCLUSION

Traces Visible to Those Who Know Where to Look

A Guide to Spotting Claremont's Legacy

> We have it within ourselves, X-Men—as do all people, whether mutants or no—to leave our world better than we found it. To strive for the height of our potential, to seek out the best in ourselves and in others.
> —Chris Claremont ("Fallout!")

In Your Cinema

In 1982, Claremont drafted a thirty-page film treatment for *X-Men: The Movie* subtitled "Rite of Passage" (Papers). The story focuses on the introduction of Kitty Pryde to the X-Men and on a battle with Proteus that would take place primarily on the astral plane. The first lines of the treatment state, "This is the story of a young woman's coming of age—of how five disparate individuals are forged into a team of heroes, and of how Kitty Pryde comes to be a part of that team." It was never produced, nor were a number of other proposed *X-Men* adaptations (many of which Claremont played a part in) during his initial time on *X-Men* comics.

In his 2019 introduction to the *Marvel Visionaries: Chris Claremont* trade, Marvel editor in chief C. B. Cebulski suggests a specific link between Claremont's style of writing and the twentieth-century wave of superhero films: "With super hero adventures now flying into movie theatres, Chris's work has become something of a standard for much of what Hollywood puts on the big screen. His comics, with their intricate character dynamics and interpersonal relationships, have become the source that many Tinseltown writers and directors pull from to make their characters speak and act like modern-day heroes should" (n.p.). In this sense, it is possible to see Claremont's style of comics writing providing something of a bridge between the two media forms: a comic that speaks the language of film at the level of character and relationships.

Yet despite his rather large storytelling contribution to the X-Men film franchise that was produced, Claremont has not always received his due. As of 2023, Claremont has eleven credits as a writer on IMDb—none of them for the X-Men film franchise that has generated six billion dollars in profit, despite the fact that at least seven of the thirteen films draw directly on storylines that he created. This is not to mention, of course, the character cultivation, dynamics, premises, and settings that inform the less-literal adaptations, but of course intellectual property law is largely incapable of quantifying such abstract properties. Claremont does receive credits for "characters" on the first two X-Men films. Otherwise, he is formally acknowledged through "thanks" in the credits and even with a few cameo appearances in the films, both systems of accreditation that cost the filmmakers very very little and that fail to acknowledge him as a creator. On the other hand, and to the great credit of the show's creators, Claremont was credited as a writer for multiple episodes of *X-Men: The Animated Series* whenever stories drew directly on his work.

In Your Streaming Series

That bridging mentality can be just as easily applied to streaming television. In a 2019 essay for *The Conversation*, I argued the following:

> Claremont's techniques are widely visible among the best-loved television series within this current golden age: nested story

structures, drawn-out mysteries, character melodrama and dysfunctional collectives that have to put aside their differences to defeat a common foe.... His greatest accomplishment—developing ways by which a character-based story could unfold slowly over time—was, ironically, what cost him his job. But if our current television landscape is any indication, our culture has profited greatly from the choices Claremont made, and from the ingenuity that followed those choices. ("How an X-Men Writer" n.p.)

We see a lot of Claremont (including direct references) in the works of some of the chief architects of long-form televisual storytelling, such as Joss Whedon, the Duffer Brothers, and George R. R. Martin. As Geoff Klock notes, Claremont's influence "looms too large for many to see" (2).

In Your Video Games

In 1989, LJN released their infamous *X-Men* video game, which is, to this day, considered one of the worst video games in the history of the original Nintendo console. All in all, the game represents a long-standing problem with licensed video game transmediations: an interest in selling an intellectual property without appreciating or engaging with the mythology surrounding it. We would get good X-Men games in the future (sometimes even very good), but this was the first and one of just three to be published during the time of Claremont's original run.

But there have been forty more since. *X-Men Legends* (2006) alone sold two million units and is widely regarded as a highpoint for the medium. In consequence, Claremont's stories and characters have found footing in the video game industry.

In Your Poetry

In "The Poetics of Fandom: The X-Men Persona Poems of Gary Jackson and Stephanie Burt," author Xander Gershberg reviews a pair of collections by prominent poets who were inspired to write about X-Men rather than roses or tygers. Gershberg argues, "Jackson and Burt's poems together are using the ekphrastic tradition to transform understandings of Marvel superheroes" (n.p.). While Gershberg fails in this article by envisioning this relationship between comics about X-Men and poetry about X-Men as a metaphorical "glow up," the simple point that world-class poets are writing poems about Claremont characters and concepts is noteworthy, and the fact that scholars such as Gershberg fail to recognize the power of the source material in that configuration is itself testament to the further ways that Claremont has been denied his dues in yet another media format.

On Your Playgrounds

How Claremont's portrayals influenced our broader culture is hard to define, but there is one study that speaks to the influence his works may have had (through the animated series) on empowering young children to diversify their imaginative play during recess. In 1994, at the peak of the popularity of *X-Men: The Animated Series*, scholar Anne Haas Dyson conducted an ethnography looking at X-Men role-playing in the recess culture of one primary school. Dyson's observations are couched in the theories of Mikhail Bakhtin. She notes, "As Bakhtin argued, the stories we tell not only shape a specific ongoing relationship . . . they also dynamically reveal our response to broader, deeper cultural conversations" (n.p.) such as gender, strength, and race. In Dyson's observations, the most popular recess imaginative play at the time was based on either X-Men or Ninja Turtles, but the Ninja Turtles kids seemed to exclude women participants and X-Men didn't: "Indeed, all children familiar with the superhero stories agreed that both girls and boys are on the X-Men team. Moreover, they knew too that, in Sammy's words, the X-Men women are 'as strong as men.' Further, X-Men stories emphasize mental as well as physical strength; in fact, Professor X, the leader of the X-Men, is in a wheelchair. Thus, the girls had new grounds for demanding inclusion" (n.p.). Dyson's overarching conclusion is that "the X-Men play, then, raised the possibility of new images of gender and of power" (n.p.). More specifically, Dyson recounts how two particular girls broke off and started their own X-Men game. And though they fought over who got to be Rogue, in their vision, "superhero teams were dominated by women of color, who nonetheless, served with women and men of different races. Moreover, power itself was tempered with human fragility: People fought, became tired, grieved, and died. These two activist girls—experienced writers of relationships—were changing the possibilities for superhero stories in the local culture of the classroom" (n.p.).

Thus, in this one second-grade classroom (which may or may not be representative of a great many classrooms), we get an example of how some of Claremont's progressive ideas permeated the popular culture and made a very real difference in the lives of children, or perhaps even a generation of children.

In Summation, Then

It is very nearly impossible to measure the sphere of influence of the stories and characters that came out of the mind of Chris Claremont, but it is safe to say (quite evident even) that they have generated billions of dollars and inspired generations of readers, fans, creators, and (yes) scholars. To know the life and work of Christopher S. Claremont is to know something important about the world that we live in and, quite especially, about the stories that we tell.

ACKNOWLEDGMENTS

This book was made possible by the support and vision of Frederick Aldama, Lisa McMurtray, and everyone at the University Press of Mississippi. I must also thank St. Jerome's University for their constant support of both me as a scholar and of the weird comics projects that I keep throwing at them. Additionally, I would like to acknowledge the great personal support of Ren Grafton, Veronica Austen, Diana Lobb, Matt Poulter, Liam Gardner, and, of course, John and Penny Deman. I love you all. Lastly, I think this book is itself an acknowledgment of Chris Claremont but it merits repeating: thank you for your work and thank you especially for characters who can make the world itself a little less lonely.

NOTES

INTRODUCTION

1. Where that book, recipient of the 2024 Eisner Award for Best Academic/Scholarly Work, focused specifically on Claremont's progressive portrayal of gender in the pages of *Uncanny X-Men*, this book focuses on a more holistic view of Claremont's career and writing strategies.

2. By eroding the concept of superhero plot armor, Jean's death is often noted by scholars as having "infused the series with a sense of danger and surprise" (Lowder 53).

3. Scholar Jeffrey A. Brown notes that "X-Men challenged the conventional depiction of heroic men and women as flawless gender ideals" (10).

CHAPTER 1: THAT ACTOR/INTERN: EARLY LIFE AND BEGINNING OF MARVEL CAREER

1. Claremont would canonically identify the address of the X-Mansion in *Uncanny X-Men* as 1407 Graymalkin Lane.

2. Claremont would later make the heroine Jean Grey's father a member of the Bard College Faculty in the pages of X-Men comics.

3. Scholar andré carrington argues that Misty Knight can be read as an important supplement to Claremont's much-heralded representation of a Black female superhero in the X-Men's Storm. For carrington, Misty and Storm can be juxtaposed with each other in meaningful ways, as a result of occupying the same fictional universe, with "Misty Knight reinforcing recognizable iterations of Blackness and Storm displacing them" (101).

CHAPTER 2: NOBODY CARED WHAT WE WERE DOING: THE COCKRUM AND BYRNE YEARS

1. We should also note that the Phoenix's arrival directly coincides with the arrival of another enigmatic cosmic being: Lilandra, a deposed empress from a distant galactic empire, and while their respective arrivals are basically unrelated to each other, it would be quite logical for a reader to assume the opposite, thus enhancing the overarching intrigue.

2. "The new *X-Men* quickly became Marvel's most popular title—both in terms of sales and critical appreciation" (Reynolds, *Super Heroes* 85).

3. Mystique has been singled out by comics scholars for her queer potential to speak to both lesbianism and transsexuality. Jeffrey A. Brown notes, "Mystique's powers are formidable and could offer a utopian model for imagining trans possibilities in the media" (153), and though Brown finds that this depiction is complicated by her villain coding, Claremont would later transition the character into an antihero.

4. Douglas Wolk reads the potential symbolism like this: "The empowerment of women is so dangerous to patriarchal culture that it will systematically destroy a woman who claims power for herself" (153), a dark and incisive critique of patriarchal culture.

CHAPTER 3: THE LONG GAME: THE SMITH AND ROMITA ERA

1. Claremont was not a fan of this Magneto as a character, describing him as a "simple, basic, traditional comic book villain, the X-Men's equivalent of Doctor Doom for the Fantastic Four, or the Green Goblin for Spider-Man" ("No Straw Dogs Here" 8).

2. In a classic Marvel bait and switch to align with the values of the company and the strictures of the comics code, it is revealed in the next issue that Callisto miraculously survived the stabbing, but the story in this issue very much suggests that Callisto was killed by Storm.

3. According to Louise Simonson, the "Mutant Massacre" was largely the product of a simple miscommunication between Claremont and illustrator Paul Smith, one that demanded a radical correction. "Chris asked Paul to draw the alley—the place where the mutant Morlocks gathered. I think Chris figured there were maybe a couple of hundred, maybe 300 Morlocks altogether. Anyway, Paul drew a crowd. He drew huge numbers of mutants thronging the alley. There must have been thousands. Chris eventually said this really was too many mutants, and decided there was going to be this 'Mutant Massacre'" (qtd. in DeFalco 144).

4. Dazzler was designed to be a comic book, album, and movie (starring sex symbol Bo Derek) all at the same time. This highly ambitious plan failed when Marvel's partners were unable to finance their ends, and Dazzler became just a comic character. She debuted in a cameo during "The Dark Phoenix Saga," and thus Claremont was the first to write her (though not her creator). She bounced around Marvel guest roles, then had a solo series and Marvel graphic novel (with tremendous cover art). Nothing caught on.

CHAPTER 4: MUTANT MITOSIS: THE X SPIN-OFFS

1. In the opening page of the Magik miniseries, she specifically states that she was "consort to a devil" (Claremont, *Little Girl Lost*).

2. It is also worth noting that the film took the subtextual queer relationship between Rahne Sinclair and Dani Moonstar and made it textual.

CHAPTER 5: TWO INFERNOS: THE SILVESTRI AND LEE YEARS AND THE DEPARTURE

1. Powell calls Inferno "a culmination, this time of major long-running plot threads. A massive amount of momentum comes to a breathtaking finale over the course of 1988" (217).

2. Jason Powell suggests that Claremont was obliged by Marvel editorial to reinstate status quo during his last ten issues on *Uncanny X-Men* (236).

CHAPTER 6: RETURNING LEGEND:
SUBSEQUENT RETURNS AND OTHER NOTABLE WORKS

1. Claremont describes the FF as "the heroes who, under the creative hands of Stan Lee and Jack Kirby, caught my eye and heart back in high school with the arrival on Earth of the Watcher, the Silver Surfer and Galactus" ("Introduction" 5).

WORKS CITED

Avila, Mike. "Master Inker Scott Williams on Inking Jim Lee & X-Men Deadline Woes." *SYFY Official Site*, 16 Oct. 2020, https://www.syfy.com/syfywire/scott-williams-on-inking-jim-lee-x-men-deadlines.

Barnhardt, Adam. "Marvel Legend Roy Thomas on His Storied Comics Career, the Future of Comic Book Movies, and More." *Comicbook*, 2 Nov. 2021, https://comicbook.com/marvel/news/marvel-legend-roy-thomas-on-his-storied-comics-career-the-future-of-comic-book-movies-and-more/.

Berlatsky, Noah. *Wonder Woman: Bondage and Feminism in the Marston/Peter Comics, 1941–1948*. Rutgers, 2015.

Boone, Josh, director. *The New Mutants*. Walt Disney Studios, 2020.

Booy, Miles. *Marvel's Mutants: The X-Men Comics of Chris Claremont*. I. B. Tauris, 2018.

Brown, Jeffrey A. *Love, Sex, Gender, and Super-Heroes*. Rutgers, 2022.

Bukatman, Scott. *Matters of Gravity: Special Effects and Supermen in the 20th Century*. Duke University Press, 2003.

Burt, Stephanie. "Prayer for Werewolves." *For All Mutants*, OHM, 2021, p. 7.

Caillava, Marie-Catherine. "Magneto the Jew." *The Unauthorized X-Men*, edited by Len Wein, Smart Pop, 2005, pp. 99–112.

Caldas, Carlos. "Comic Books as a Theological Discourse: An Analysis of X Men—God Loves, Man Kills, by Chris Claremont from the Perspective of Paul Tillich's Soteriology." *Teoliteraria*, vol. 7, no. 14, 2017, pp. 71–90.

Campochiaro, Michael, "On X-(Wo)Men and Third-Wave Feminism." Sequart Organization, 6 Feb. 2016, http://sequart.org/magazine/62699/on-x-women-and-third-wave-feminism/.

Carnes, Jeremy M. "The Original Enchantment: Whiteness, Indigeneity, and Representational Logics in *The New Mutants*." *Unstable Masks: Whiteness and American Superhero Comics*, edited by Sean Guynes and Martin Lund, Ohio State UP, 2020, pp. 57–71.

carrington, andré m. *Speculative Blackness: The Future of Race in Science Fiction*. U of Minnesota P, 2016.

CBR staff. "Bill Sienkiewicz Interview." *CBR*, 17 Jul. 2001, https://www.cbr.com/bill-sienkiewicz-interview/.

Cebulski, C. B. "Introduction." *Marvel Visionaries: Chris Claremont*. Marvel, 2019.

Claremont, Chris. "The Action of the Tiger." *Uncanny X-Men*, vol. 1, no. 128, Marvel, 1979.

Claremont, Chris. "And Hellfire Is Their Name." *Uncanny X-Men*, vol. 1, no. 132, Marvel, 1980.

Claremont, Chris. "Armageddon Now." *Uncanny X-Men*, vol. 1, no. 108, Marvel, 1977.

Claremont, Chris. *The Black Dragon*. Titan Comics, 2014.

Claremont, Chris. "By Friends—Betrayed!" *Avengers Annual*, vol. 1, no. 10, Marvel, 1981.

Claremont, Chris. "Cry for the Children!" *Uncanny X-Men*, vol. 1, no. 122, Marvel, 1979.

Claremont, Chris. "Dancin' in the Dark." *Uncanny X-Men*, vol. 1, no. 170, Marvel, 1983.

Claremont, Chris. "Deathstar, Rising!" *Uncanny X-Men*, vol. 1, no. 99, Marvel, 1976.

Claremont, Chris. "Demon." *Uncanny X-Men*, vol. 1, no. 143, Marvel, 1981.

Claremont, Chris. "Down Under." *Uncanny X-Men*, vol. 1, no. 229, Marvel, 1988.

Claremont, Chris. "Elegy." *Uncanny X-Men*, vol. 1, no. 138, Marvel, 1980.

Claremont, Chris. "End of Days." *X-Men*, vol. 2, no. 100, Marvel, 2000.

Claremont, Chris. "Fallout!" *X-Men*, vol. 2, no. 3, Marvel, 1991.

Claremont, Chris. "The Fate of the Phoenix!" *Uncanny X-Men*, vol. 1, no. 137, Marvel, 1980.

Claremont, Chris. "Fever Dream." *Uncanny X-Men*, vol. 1, no. 251, Marvel, 1989.

Claremont, Chris. *God Loves Man Kills*. 2nd ed., Marvel Worldwide, 2011.

Claremont, Chris. "The Goth." *X-Men*, vol. 2, no. 103, Marvel, 2000.

Claremont, Chris. "Greater Love Hath No X-Man. . . ." *X-Men*, vol. 1, no. 100, Marvel, 1976.

Claremont, Chris. "He Only Laughs When I Hurt!" *Uncanny X-Men*, vol. 1, no. 124, Marvel, 1979.

Claremont, Chris. "Hope." *Classic X-Men*, vol. 1, no. 11, Marvel, 1987.

Claremont, Chris. "I Am Wolverine." *Wolverine*, vol. 1, no. 1, Marvel, 1982.

Claremont, Chris. "Introduction." *Captain Britain*, by Alan Davis and Jamie Delano, Marvel Comics, 1988, pp. 5–8.

Claremont, Chris. "Introduction." *Marvel Universe by Chris Claremont*. Marvel Comics, 2017, p. 5.

Claremont, Chris. "Introduction to New Mutants #45." *New Mutants Omnibus*, vol. 2, by Chris Claremont et al., Marvel, 2022, n.p.

Claremont, Chris. "Introduction to X-Men: Vignettes." *X-Men: Vignettes*. Marvel Comics, 2001.

Claremont, Chris. "Ladies Night." *Uncanny X-Men*, vol. 1, no. 244, Marvel, 1989.

Claremont, Chris. "Lifedeath." *Uncanny X-Men*, vol. 1, no. 186, Marvel, 1984.

Claremont, Chris. "Listen—Stop Me If You've Heard It—But This One Will Kill You!" *Uncanny X-Men*, vol. 1, no. 123, Marvel, 1979.

Claremont, Chris. "Little Girl Lost." *Magik*, vol. 1, no. 1, Marvel, 1983.

Claremont, Chris. "A Lost Soul." *Uncanny X-Men Omnibus*, vol. 5, by Chris Claremont et al., Marvel, 2022, pp. 312–13.

Claremont, Chris. "Madness." *Uncanny X-Men*, vol. 1, no. 182, Marvel, 1984.
Claremont, Chris. *Marada the She-Wolf*. Marvel Comics Group, 1985.
Claremont, Chris. "Men!" *Uncanny X-Men*, vol. 1, no. 245, Marvel, 1989.
Claremont, Chris. "Mindgames." *Uncanny X-Men*, vol. 1, no. 111, Marvel, 1984.
Claremont, Chris. "No Straw Dogs Here." *Uncanny X-Men Omnibus*, vol. 5, by Chris Claremont et al., Marvel, 2022, pp. 8–9.
Claremont, Chris. "Omens and Portents." *Uncanny X-Men*, vol. 1, no. 223, Marvel, 1987.
Claremont, Chris. Papers, 1973–2018. Rare Manuscript Collection, Rare Book and Manuscript Library, Columbia University, New York. Accessed 20 May 2019.
Claremont, Chris. Personal interview 1. 19 May 2014.
Claremont, Chris. Personal interview 2. 19 May 2014.
Claremont, Chris. "Resurrection." *Uncanny X-Men* Annual, vol. 1, no. 12, Marvel, 1988.
Claremont, Chris. "Rogue Storm!" *Uncanny X-Men*, vol. 1, no. 147, Marvel, 1981.
Claremont, Chris. "Scarlet in Glory." *Uncanny X-Men*, vol. 1, no. 172, Marvel, 1983.
Claremont, Chris. "The Sword Is Drawn." *Excalibur: Special Edition*, vol. 1, no. 1, Marvel, 1987.
Claremont, Chris. "The Tenth Circle." *JLA*, vol. 1, no. 94, DC, 2004.
Claremont, Chris. "This One's for You!" *X-Men Unlimited*, vol. 1, no. 36, Marvel, 2002.
Claremont, Chris. "To Save the Savage Land." *Uncanny X-Men*, vol. 1, no. 116, Marvel, 1978.
Claremont, Chris. "The Trial of Magneto!" *Uncanny X-Men*, vol. 1, no. 200, Marvel, 1985.
Claremont, Chris. "War Children." *New Mutants: War Children*, vol. 1, no.1, Marvel, 2019.
Claremont, Chris. "Way of the Warrior." *The New Mutants*, vol. 1, no. 41, Marvel, 1986.
Claremont, Chris. "Who Will Stop the Juggernaut?" *X-Men*, vol. 1, no. 102, Marvel, 1976.
Claremont, Chris. "Why Do We Do These Things We Do?" *New Mutants Annual*, vol. 1, no. 2, Marvel, 1986.
Cocca, Carolyn. *Superwomen: Gender, Power, and Representation*. Bloomsbury Academic, 2016.
Cooper, Carol. "Leading by Example: The Tao of Women in the X-Men World." *The Unauthorized X-Men*, edited by Len Wein, Smart Pop, 2005, pp. 183–200.
Cronin, Brian. "Revisiting Chris Claremont's Sovereign Seven." *CBR*, 14 Apr. 2018, https://www.cbr.com/sovereign-seven-chris-claremont-dc-comics/.
D'Agostino, Anthony Michael. "'Flesh to Flesh Contact': Marvel Comics' Rogue and the Queer Feminist Imagination." *American Literature*, vol. 90, no. 2, 2018, pp. 251–282.
Darius, Julian. "Alan Moore's Miracleman and the Influence of Chris Claremont's Dark Phoenix Saga." *Sequart Organization*, 30 Apr. 2012. http://sequart.org/magazine/11190/alan-moores-miracleman-book-one-and-the-influence-of-chris-claremonts-dark-phoenix-saga/.

Darowski, Joseph J. *X-Men and the Mutant Metaphor: Race and Gender in the Comic Books*. Rowman and Littlefield, 2014.

"Dave Cockrum's Outsiders." *Cosmic Teams!*, https://www.cosmicteams.com/legion/docs/theoutsiders.html.

Davis, Alan. "Introduction by Alan Davis from X-Men: Danger Room Battle Archives TPB (1996)." *Uncanny X-Men Omnibus*, vol. 5. by Chris Claremont et al., Marvel, 2022, supplemental material.

Davis, Alan. "It's Hard to Be a Hero." *Captain Britain*, vol. 2, no. 13, Marvel, 1986.

DeFalco, Tom. *Comics Creators on X-Men*. Titan, 2006.

Deman, J. Andrew. *The Claremont Run: Subverting Gender in the X-Men*. U Texas P, 2023.

Deman, J. Andrew. "How an X-Men Writer Inspired Binge-Worthy, Character-Driven TV from *Buffy* to *Game of Thrones*." *The Conversation*, 27 Sept. 2023, theconversation.com/how-an-x-men-writer-inspired-binge-worthy-character-driven-tv-from-buffy-to-game-of-thrones-110764.

Dyson, Anne Haas. "The Ninjas, the X-Men, and the Ladies: Playing with Power and Identity in an Urban Primary School." *Teachers College Record*, vol. 96, no. 2, pp. 219–39.

Edidin, Jay and Miles Stokes. "Jay and Miles XPlain the X-Men," https://www.xplainthexmen.com/.

Fawaz, Ramzi. *The New Mutants: Superheroes and the Radical Imagination of American Comics*. New York UP, 2016.

Fingeroth, Danny. *Disguised As Clark Kent: Jews, Comics, and the Creation of the Superhero*. Continuum, 2007.

Foege, Alec. "The X-Men Files—Nymag." *New York Magazine*, 11 Apr. 2019, https://nymag.com/nymetro/arts/features/3522/.

G, Mady and J. R. Zuckerberg. *A Quick & Easy Guide to Queer & Trans Identities*. Limerence Press, 2019.

Galvan, Margaret. "From Kitty to Cat: Kitty Pryde and the Phases of Feminism." *The Ages of the X-Men: Essays on the Children of the Atom in Changing Times*, edited by Joseph J. Darowski, McFarland, 2014, pp. 46–62.

Gershberg, Xander. "The Poetics of Fandom: The X-Men Persona Poems of Gary Jackson and Stephanie Burt." *The Minnesota Review*, 7 Nov. 2021, https://minnesotareview.wordpress.com/2021/11/07/the-poetics-of-fandom-the-x-men-persona-poems-of-gary-jackson-and-stephanie-burt.

Gorton, Austin. "X-Amining X-Men (Vol. 2) #3." *Gentlemen of Leisure*, 1 June 2016, https://www.therealgentlemenofleisure.com/2016/06/x-amining-x-men-vol-2-3.html.

Haraway, Donna. "A Cyborg Manifesto: Science, Technology, and Socialist-Feminism in the Late Twentieth Century." *Simians, Cyborgs and Women: The Reinvention of Nature*, Routledge, 1991, pp. 149–81.

Hembeck, Fred. "The Mutant Report." *Marvel Age*, vol. 1, no. 69, Marvel, 1988.

Holm, Nicholas. "Excalibur, Aesthetics and an Other Britain: From Whimsical Tradition to Tabloid Aesthetic." *Journal of Graphic Novels and Comics*, vol. 12, no. 5, 2021, pp. 912–23.
Howe, Sean. *Marvel Comics: The Untold Story*. Harper, 2013.
"I'm Chris Claremont and I wrote the X-Men for over 17 years at Marvel Comics, including the Dark Phoenix Saga and Days of Future Past. AMA!" 19 Nov. 2020, https://www.reddit.com/r/comicbooks/comments/jx6pjr/im_chris_claremont_and_i_wrote_the_xmen_for_over/.
"Interview with Roger Stern." *Marvel Masterworks Resource Page,* www.marvelessentials.com/features/int_stern_1006_3.html.
"Jay & Miles X-Plain the X-Men." *Men,* 17 Sept. 2023, www.xplainthexmen.com/.
"Jim Shooter Biographical Interview by Alex Grand & Jim Thompson—Comic Book Historians." *Comic Book Historians—An Online Fanzine,* 24 June 2023, https://comicbookhistorians.com/jim-shooter-biographical-interview-by-alex-grand-jim-thompson/.
Johnson, Derek. "Franchise Histories: Marvel, *X-Men*, and the Negotiated Process of Expansion." *Convergence Media History,* edited by Janet Staiger and Sabine Hake, Routledge, 2009, pp. 14–23.
Klock, Geoff. "On Chris Clairmont's X-Men." *The Best There Is at What He Does: Examining Chris Claremont's X-Men,* by Jason Powel, Sequart, 2016, pp. 1–7.
Kte'pi, Bill. "An Appreciation of Chris Claremont's Fantastic Four." *How To Love Comics,* 2 May 2021, https://www.howtolovecomics.com/2021/05/02/chris-claremont-fantastic-four/.
Langsdale, Sam. *Searching for Feminist Superheroes*. U Texas P, 2024.
Laub, Dori. "Holocaust Survivors: Adaptation to Trauma." *Patterns of Prejudice,* vol. 13, no. 1, 1979, pp. 17–25.
Lee, Stan. "To Set the Style." *The Uncanny X-Men Omnibus,* vol. 1, by Chris Claremont et. al, Marvel, 2016, pp. 378–9.
Lowder, James. "Infinite Mutation, Eternal Stasis," in *The Unauthorized X-Men,* edited by Len Wein, Smart Pop, 2005, pp. 51–64.
McDaniel, Anita. "Negotiating Life Spaces: How Marriage Marginalized Storm," in *Heroines of Comic Books and Literature, Portrayals in Popular Culture,* edited by Maja Bajac-Carter, Norma Jones, and Bob Batchelor, Lanham, Rowman & Littlefield, 2014, pp. 119–32.
Moore, Alan. *Watchmen*. New, collected edition. DC Comics, 2019.
Morrison, Grant. *Supergods*. Spiegel & Grau, 2011.
Murray, Ross. "The Feminine Mystique: Feminism, Sexuality, Motherhood," *Journal of Graphic Novels and Comics,* vol. 2, no. 1, 2011, pp. 55–66.
Nocenti, Ann. "Introduction by Ann Nocenti from Longshot TPB (1989)." *Uncanny X-Men Omnibus,* vol. 5. by Chris Claremont et al., Marvel, 2022, supplemental material.

Peppard, Anna F. "'Til Death Do We Part, at Least for a While: My Undying Love Affair with Undying Superheroes." *The Vault of Culture*, 16 Apr. 2020, https://www.vaultofculture.com/vault/feature/peppard/undying.

Powell, Jason. *The Best There Is at What He Does: Examining Chris Claremont's X-Men*. Sequart, 2016.

Reynolds, Richard. "Emma Frost, The White Queen: Superpowers as the Performance of Gender." *Toxic Masculinity: Mapping the Monstrous in Our Heroes*, edited by Esther De Dauw and Daniel J. Connell, UP of Mississippi, 2020, pp. 121–41.

Reynolds, Richard. *Super Heroes: A Modern Mythology*. UP of Mississippi, 1994.

Riesman, Abraham Josephine. "Meet the Underappreciated Woman Who Invented X-Men's Apocalypse." *Vulture*, 31 May 2016, https://www.vulture.com/2016/05/louise-simonson-fox-apocalypse.html.

Sabin, Roger. *Comics, Comix and Graphic Novels*. Phaidon, 2014.

Sanderson, Peter. *The X-Men Companion II*, Fantagraphics Books, 1982.

Scott Darieck and Ramzi Fawaz. "Introduction: Queer About Comics." *American Literature*, vol. 90, no. 2, 2018, pp. 197–220.

Shcherbenok, Andrey. "Asymmetric Warfare: The Vision of the Enemy in American and Soviet Cold War Cinemas." *KinoKultura*, vol. 28, no. 1, 2010, pp. 1–13.

Simone, Gail. "Women in Refrigerators." *Lby3.com*, 1999, http://www.lby3.com/wir/.

Singer, Mark. "Superheroes." *Comics Studies: A Guidebook*, Rutgers, 2020, pp. 213–26.

Smith, Travis. *Superhero Ethics*. Templeton, 2019.

Spurgeon, Tom. "Dave Cockrum, 1943–2006." *The Comics Reporter*, 1 Dec. 2006, https://www.comicsreporter.com/index.php/resources/longbox/6958.

Thomas, Roy. "Do or Die, Baby!" *X-Men*, vol. 1, no. 59. Marvel, 1969.

Thompson, Kim. "Kim Thompson Interview." *Paul Smith*, 12 Sept. 2018, https://paulmartinsmith.com/content/kim-thompson-interview.

Valiente, Doreen. *The Rebirth of Witchcraft*. Phoenix Pub, 1989.

Werbe, Charlotte F. "Retroactive Continuity, Holocaust Testimony, and X-Men's Magneto." *The Journal of Holocaust Research*, vol. 33, no. 4, 2019, pp. 302–13.

Whaley, Deborah E. *Black Women in Sequence: Re-inking Comics, Graphic Novels, and Anime*. U of Washington P, 2016.

Wolk, Douglas. *All of the Marvels: A Journey to the Ends of the Biggest Story Ever Told*. Penguin Press, 2021.

Zigarovich, Jolene. "The Trans Legacy of *Frankenstein*." *Science Fiction Studies*, vol. 45, no. 2, 2018, pp. 260–72, https://doi.org/10.5621/sciefictstud.45.2.0260.

Zimmerman, Dwight Jon. "Alan Davis on Excalibur." *Excalibur: Epic Collection: The Sword Is Drawn*, by Chris Claremont, Marvel Universe, 2022.

INDEX

Page numbers in *italics* indicate a figure.

Adams, Arthur, 5, 75, 96
Adams, Neal, 5, 56
Alison/Dazzler, 75, 103, 130n4 (chap. 3)
Archangel, 102
art: cinematic style, 34, 105–6; individualizing and humanizing characters, 34, 53; Outback era, 99–101; Smith and Romita era, 53–56; storytelling enhanced by, 34–36, 53, 55–56, 59, 85, 92, 96; text in tension with, 116; visual experimentation, 56, 83–85. *See also individual artists*
Austin, Terry, 34, *35*
Avengers Annual, no. 10 "By Friends—Betrayed!," 26, 61
aviation, 20–21

Bakhtin, Mikhail, 125
Banshee, 37, 104
Bard College, 22–24, 129n2 (chap. 1)
BDSM symbolism: author's overview, 15–17; Hellfire Club, 15–16, *16*, 50–51; villainy signalled by, 15, 112; Wonder Woman, 17. *See also* queer representation; sex and sexuality
Berlatsky, Noah, 17
Betsy Braddock/Psylocke/Captain Britain, 75–76, 103
Black Dragon, The, 26–27

Bolton, John, 26–27, 96
Bonnie Wilford/Graymalkin, 22
Brian Braddock/Captain Britain, 8, 25, 91, 93–94
Brown, Jeffrey A., 129n3 (intro), 130n3 (chap. 2)
Bukatman, Scott, 13, 20
Burt, Stephanie, 13
Buscema, John, 5
Busiek, Kurt, 49
Butler, Judith, 12
Byrne, John: cinematic approach of, 34, 106; collaboration with Claremont, 33–34, *35*, 36–37, 51; "The Dark Phoenix Saga" storyline, 47, 51; Hellfire Club, *16*; *Iron Fist*, 25; Wolverine, 40–41

Caillava, Marie-Catherine, 59–60
Caldas, Carlos, 52–53
Callisto, 67–69, *68*, 130n2 (chap. 3)
Campochiaro, Michael, 61–62
Captain Britain, 25, 76, 89–90, 94
Captain Marvel, 20–21
Carnes, Jeremy, 38
Carol Danvers/Captain Marvel/Ms. Marvel, 20, 25–26
carrington, andré, 129n3 (chap. 1)
Cebulski, C. B., 122–23

Cecilia Reyes, 116
character depth: in Dissolution and Rebirth era, 103–5; fear, anxiety, and self-doubt, 7–9, 39–40; genre shifts and, 79–82, 89; in "Inferno" storyline, 102, 115; mortal consciousness and fear of death, 66; redemption and rehabilitation arcs, 25–26, 29–30, 59–61, 65, 75–76, 115, 130n1 (chap. 3); relatability and, 39–40, 42, 65–66, 67, 83–88; retrospective continuity and, 95–96; romantic relationships, 43–44, 56, 66–67, 71–72, 93–94, 131n2 (chap. 4); suicidal ideation, 7–8, 91; trauma, 60, 63–65, 69, 72–74, 85–86, 94, 119; vulnerability, 8, 39–40, 41–42, 47, 66, 118. *See also* gender representation; queer representation; *individual characters*
characters: Claremont's approach to, 6–8, 24, 36–37, 64; comingling characters from various titles, 30, 75–76; departure from heroic paradigms, 8–9; Indigenous characters, 37–38, 86–88; mutant body's emancipatory potential, 12–13; relatable symbolism, 39–42, 47, 66; self-definition in resistance to external forces, 14; Stan Lee on *UXM* characters, 7. *See also* art; character depth; progressive representation; *individual characters*
Charles Xavier/Professor X, 60–61
Charlotte Jones, 116
Claremont, Chris: childhood, 20; comparison to Steven Spielberg, 3; as difficult to work with, 58; early career portfolio, 23–27; economic success, 4; education, 22–24, 129n2 (chap. 1); legacy beyond comics, 122–26; novel writing, 111; parents' influence, 20–21, 76; popular appeal of work, 3; potentially negative quirks, 6; religion and faith, 21–22; suicidal ideation, 23. *See also* characters; collaborations; long-form storytelling; Marvel Comics; progressive representation; *Uncanny X-Men*; X-Men comics
Classic X-Men: author's overview, 94–95; no. 11 "Hope," 8; no. 21 "Visions of Death!," 95; no. 22 "To Save the Savage Land," 95; retrospective continuity, 95–96
Cocca, Carolyn, 11, 38
Cockrum, Dave: contributions to *UXM*, 31, 32–33; *Giant-Size X-Men*, 28; Nightcrawler, 42; on Thunderbird's death, 38
Cold War, 44–45
collaborations: art and text in tension, 116; central to success, 4–6, 32–33; Claremont paying collaborators out of pocket, 36; editorial collaboration, 56–59; storytelling enhanced by artists, 34–36, 53, 55–56, 59, 85, 92, 96. *See also* art; Byrne, John; Cockrum, Dave; Davis, Alan
Colleen Wing, 25
Cooper, Carol, 10, 20, 65–66
Cronin, Brian, 112

D'Agostino, Anthony Michael, 62–63
Dani Moonstar/Mirage, 83, 86–88, 131n2 (chap. 4)
Darieck, Scott, 11
Darius, Julian, 47
Darowski, Joe, 116
Davis, Alan: *Captain Britain*, 25, 76, 90; *Excalibur*, 27, 92, 93; *New Mutants Annual*, 76

DC Comics, 8–9, 111, 112–13
DeConnick, Kelley Sue, 20
Delano, Jamie, 25, 76, 90
Deman, Andrew, 123–24
Deppey, Dirk, 114
Destiny, 43–44, 56
Dini, Paul, 94
Ditko, Steve, 53
Drake, Arnold, 5
Duffer Brothers, 124
Dyson, Anne Haas, 125–26

ecofeminism, 40
Edidin, Jay, 52
Ellis, Warren, 118
Emma Frost, 50
Epic Comics, 26–27
Excalibur: The Black Dragon and, 27; *Captain Britain* mythology, 89–90, 94; "The Cross-Time Caper" storyline, 92–93; dysfunctional coupling in, 93–94; Kitty Pryde's evolution, 118; no. 3 "Moving Day," 93; Rachel Summers's return in, 65; as sexually charged tragicomedy, 90, 91; simulacrum of Britain, 92–93; suicidal ideation foundational to, 8, 91

families: family obligation and leadership, 69; found family, 11–12, 41, 104–5, 112; fractured biological families, 11–12, 21
fan letters and responses: to "The Dark Phoenix Saga," 49; to Thunderbird's death, 38
Fantastic Four, 113–14, 131n1 (chap. 6)
Fawaz, Ramzi, 11
female characters. *See* characters; gender representation; queer representation; sex and sexuality; *individual characters*

feminist storytelling: author's overview, 9–10; Claremont's mother's influence, 20–21; comics industry out of touch, 10; intersectionality, 14, 46; Kitty Pryde's transgressive gender politics, 45–46. *See also* gender representation
Fingeroth, Danny, 22
Foege, Alec, 24, 113
Forge, 70–71, 104
Frazetta, Frank, 99

G, Mady, 12
Galvan, Margaret, 45–46, 47
Gambit, 105
gender representation: aviation backgrounds for female characters, 20–21; Claremont's progressive approach to, 10; as conscious undertaking by Claremont, 9–10; heroism and, 125–26, 129n3 (chap. 1); inclusivity and childhood play, 125–26; patriarchal culture critiqued, 130n4 (chap. 2); progressive representations of women, 21, 25–26, 38–39, 50, 69; queering of gender roles, 62; redemption and rehabilitation of female characters, 25–26, 29–30, 61, 65, 75–76, 115; sexism, 25–26, 39, 76; teen girls, 83; transgressive gender politics of Kitty Pryde, 45–46; women's bodily agency, 61–62. *See also* BDSM symbolism; feminist storytelling; queer representation; sex and sexuality
Gershberg, Xander, 125
Giant-Size X-Men, 28–29
Gibbons, Dave, 51
God Loves, Man Kills, 52–53
good versus evil, 49–50, 52–53

Goodwin, Archie, 5
Gorton, Austin, 107
Green, Dan, 57, 77, 99

Haraway, Donna, 12–13
Harras, Bob, 107–9, 113
Havok, 75, 103
Hellfire Club, 15–16, *16*, 49–51
Hobson, Michael, 108–9
Holm, Nicholas, 92
Howard, Robert E., 26
Howe, Sean, 6, 22, 26, 56, 114
"Huntsman, The," 111, 112

illustration. *See* art
Illyana Rasputin/Magik/Darkchylde, 83, 85–86, 101, 130n1 (chap. 4)
Image Comics, 111, 112
intersectionality, 14, 46
Iron Fist, 25
Isabella, Tony, 24

Jean Grey/Phoenix: "The Dark Phoenix Saga," 48–49, 51; death of, 49, 51, 65–66, 129n2 (intro), 130n4 (chap. 2); Phoenix transformation, 29–30, *31*; resurrection in *X-Factor*, 89
John Kowalski, 24
John Proudstar/Thunderbird, 37–38
Johnson, Derek, 78–79
Jubilation Lee/Jubilee, 104–5
Judaism, 21–22, 46, 59–60
Justice League, 8–9

Karima Shapandar, 116
Karma, 83
kink. *See* BDSM symbolism
Kirby, Jack, 5, 131n1 (chap. 6)
Kitty Pryde: character progression, 116–19, *117*; debut of character, 51; first canonical Jewish superhero, 22, 46; as main viewpoint character, 46–47; as reader surrogate, 65–66, 67; "Rite of Passage" film treatment, 122; sexuality of, 66–67, 117; superhero comics landscape changed by, 45–47; transgressive gender politics, 45–46; vulnerability, 8, 66, 118
Klock, Geoff, 124
Kte'pi, Bill, 114
Kurt Wagner/Nightcrawler, 42–44, 91

Langsdale, Sam, 9
Larroca, Salvador, 5, 118
leadership, 69, 71, 73, 115
Lee, Jim, 5, 105–6, *106*, 107–9
Lee, Stan, 7, 24, 110, 131n1 (chap. 6)
Leonardi, Rick, 72, *73*
Lightle, Steve, 96
Lilandra, 129n1 (chap. 2)
Logan. *See* Wolverine/Logan
long-form storytelling: author's overview, 17–19; "The Dark Phoenix Saga," 48, 63–66; development of Kitty Pryde character and, 65–66; early examples of, 29–32; "Inferno" storyline as magnum opus, 102; influence on television series, 124; *Iron Fist*, 25; in Smith and Romita era, 52; soap opera structure of *UXM*, 52–53, 55–56, 67–74; success of, 32
Longshot, 75
love, 16, 27, 52–53
Lucasfilm, 111

Madelyne Pryor, 8, 71–72, *73*, 101
Magneto: from irredeemable villain to antihero, 59–61, 130n1 (chap. 3); in *God Loves, Man Kills*, 59; as Holocaust survivor, 22, 59–60

Marada the She-Wolf, 26
Martin, George R. R., 124
Marvel Comics: Claremont's departure from, 106–9; Claremont's early career portfolio, 23–27; Claremont's return to, 111, 113; intersection of art and commerce, 78–79, 107, 108, 110, 114, 130n2 (chap. 2). *See also* X-Men comics; *individual titles*
Marvel UK. *See Captain Britain*
McDaniels, Anita, 39
Meggan, 91, 93–94
Mignola, Mike, 96
Miller, Frank, 5, 79–80, 81
Misty Knight, 25, 129n3 (chap. 1)
Moira MacTaggert, 37
Moore, Alan: *Captain Britain*, 25, 76, 90, 94; "The Dark Phoenix Saga" and, 47, 51; *Watchmen*, 41, 51
morality, 49–50, 52–53, 69
Morlocks, 74. *See also* Callisto
Morrison, Grant, 40
mortality, 7–8, 23, 66, 91
Ms. Marvel, 25–26
Murray, Ross, 43
mutants. *See* X-bodies
Mystique, 25, 43–44, 56, 130n3 (chap. 2)

Neal Sharra/Thunderbird III, 116
New Mutants, The: didactic function, 82–83; friendship, 88; "Inferno" storyline, 101–2; racism confronted in, 82, 87–88; relatability to adolescent audiences, 83–88; surreal cosmic horror, 85
New Mutants, The, issues and storylines: no. 18 "The Demon Bear Saga," 83; no. 19 "Siege," *84*; no. 41 "Way of the Warrior," 86–87
New Mutants Annual, no. 2 "Why Do We Do These Things We Do?," 76

New Mutants: War Children, 119–21, *120*
"Nicole Shea, The" series, 20
Nocenti, Ann, 5, 58, 59, 75

Oliver, Glynnis, 5, 36, 72
Ororo Munroe/Storm: character development, 39–40, 67–71, *68*; creation of, 38; duel with Cyclops, 71, 73; ecofeminism and, 40; fear, anxiety, and vulnerability, 8, 39–40; femininity of, 69; Gamit as foil to, 105; in "Inferno" storyline, 102; juxtaposition with Misty Knight, 129n3 (chap. 1); love, 69–70; relatable symbolism and vulnerability of, 39–40; as representational milestone, 38–39; sexist tropes and, 39; trauma of leadership, 69
Orzechowski, Tom, 5, 36

Peppard, Anna, 42
Pérez, George, 5
Phoenix. *See* Jean Grey/Phoenix; Rachel Summers/Phoenix
Piotr Rasputin/Colossus, 44–45, 66–67, 103
poetry, 125
Portacio, Whilce, 72, 108, 112
Powell, Jason, 50, 98, 101, 103, 111–12, 131nn1–2 (chap. 5)
"Prayer for Werewolves," 13
progressive representation: diversity and representational politics, 13–14, 38–39, 82, 87–88, 116; morality, 49–50, 52–53, 59–61, 69, 130n1 (chap. 3); politics, 44–45. *See also* gender representation; queer representation; sex and sexuality

queer representation: author's overview, 10–12; BDSM symbolism informing, 17; Mystique and Destiny, 43–44, 56, 130n3 (chap. 2); Nightcrawler, 43–44; patriarchal values (almost) subverted, 43–44; progressive approach to, 10–12; queer mutanity, 11; Rachel Summers's visual representation, 63; Rahne Sinclair and Dani Moonstar, 131n2 (chap. 4); Rogue's queering gender roles, 62–63; Storm's punk look, 69–70, 73; trans representation, 12–13, 130n3 (chap. 2). *See also* gender representation; sex and sexuality

Rachel Summers/Phoenix, 21, 63–65, 119
Rahne Sinclair, 131n2 (chap. 2)
Red Sonja, 26
religion, 21–22, 46, 59–60
restorative justice, 61
Reynolds, Richard, 34, 50, 53
Roberto da Costa/Sunspot, 83, 88
Rogue: debut of character, 61; in Dissolution and Rebirth era, 103; dueling Wolverine for leadership of X-Men, 115; queering gender roles, 62–63; redemption arc, 61, 115; suicidal ideation, 8; women's bodily agency, 61–62
Romita, John, Jr., 5, 56, 57
Romita, John, Sr., 56

Sabin, Roger, 53
Sabretooth, 25, 119
Salicrup, Jim, 58
Sam Guthrie/Cannonball, 83, 88
Scott Summers/Cyclops, 51, 71–72, 73, 102
sex and sexuality: in *Excalibur*, 90, 91; as flagrant and subversive, 50–51; Hellfire Club, 50–51; Kitty Pryde, 66–67, 117; post-sexual violence trauma, 85–86; sexualization of superpowers, 27; women's bodily agency, 61–62. *See also* BDSM symbolism; gender representation; queer representation
Shcherbenok, Andrey, 44
Shea, Nicole, 20
Shooter, Jim, 5, 36, 56–58, 89
Sienkiewicz, Bill, 83–85, *84*, 119, *120*
Silvestri, Marc, 5, 77, 99–101, *100*
Simone, Gail, 71
Simonson, Louise, 5, 58–59, 108, 130n3 (chap. 3)
Simonson, Walt, 5
Singer, Marc, 13
Smith, Paul, 53, *54*, *68*, 130n3 (chap. 3)
Smith, Travis, 40–41
Sovereign Seven, 112–13, *113*
Spielberg, Steven, 3
Spurgeon, Tom, 32–33
Stern, Roger, 36, 58
Stokes, Miles, 52
suicidal ideation, 7–8, 23, 91
Sunfire, 37
Superman, 9

Terry and the Pirates, 89
Thomas, Roy, 5, 28, 38
Timm, Bruce, 94
trauma: hedonistic and self-destructive coping, 94; Holocaust survival and, 60; of leadership, 69; post-sexual violence, 85–86; Rachel Summers and, 63–65, 119; Storm and, 69; subversion and, 72–74
Trimpe, Herb, 25
Turner, Dwayne, *113*

Uncanny X-Men (*UXM*): bronze to modern age comics, 52–53; Claremont assigned to, 25, 28–29; creative tensions, 89, 106–9; development of new X-Men, 75–77; Dissolution and Rebirth era, 103–5; freedom to experiment, 32; Hellfire Club, 15–16, 16, 49–51; Judaism in, 22, 59–60; low sales, 28, 32; mutants in society, 49–50; Outback era, 98–103; retroactive continuity additions, 95–96; as single cohesive story, 17–18; soap opera structure, 52–53, 55–56, 67–74; spin-off series, 78–80, 82–88, 89–97; status quo reinstated, 131n2 (chap. 5). *See also* art; characters; families

Uncanny X-Men issues and storylines: "Brood Saga" storyline, 8, 66; "The Dark Phoenix Saga" storyline, 30–32, 47–51, 63–66, 102; "Days of Future Past" storyline, 46, 64; "Dissolution and Rebirth" storyline, 103–5; "End of Greys" storyline, 119; "Fall of the Mutants" storyline, 69, 76–77; "Inferno" storyline, 98–99, 101–2, 131n1 (chap. 5); "Mutant Massacre" storyline, 72–74, 130n3 (chap. 3); no. 59 "Do or Die, Baby!," 24; no. 94 "The Doomsmith Scenario!," 38; no. 95 "Warhunt!," 38; no. 97 "My Brother, My Enemy!," 29; no. 99 "Deathstar, Rising!," 43; no. 100 "Great Love Hath No X-Man . . . ," 29; no. 101 "Like a Phoenix, from the Ashes," 29–30, *31*; no. 102 "Who Will Stop the Juggernaut?," 30; no. 108 "Armageddon Now," 33–34, *35*; no. 111 "Mindgames," 18; no. 114 "The Day the X-Men Died!," 36; no. 116 "To Save the Savage Land," 40; no. 122 "Cry for the Children," 45; no. 123 "Listen—Stop Me If You've Heard It—But This One Will Kill You!," 41; no. 124 "He Only Laughs When I Hurt!," 44; no. 128 "The Action of the Tiger," 8, 41–42; no. 129 "God Spare the Child . . . ," 48; no. 132 "And Hellfire Is Their Name," 16; no. 137 "The Fate of the Phoenix!," 42, 49; no. 138 "Elegy," 51; no. 143 "Demon," 46, 49; no. 147 "Rogue Storm!," 42; no. 161 "Gold Rush!," 60; no. 168 "Professor Xavier Is a Jerk!," 54; no. 170 "Dancin' in the Dark," 16, 67–69, *68*; no. 172 "Scarlet in Glory," 69–70; no. 182 "Madness," 8; no. 183 "He'll Never Make Me Cry," 57; no. 186 "Lifedeath: A Love Story," 8, 70–71; no. 200 "The Trial of Magneto!," 60–61; no. 201 "Duel," 71, 73, 115; no. 210 "The Mutant Massacre," 56, 69; no. 223 "Omens and Portents," 8; no. 229 "Down Under," 99, *100*; no. 244 "Ladies Night," 102; no. 245 "Men!," 102; no. 251 "Fever Dream," 99; no. 256 "The Key That Breaks the Locke," 106

USSR, 44–45

War Is Hell, 24–25
Watchmen, 41, 51
Wein, Len, 5, 28–29, 38
Werbe, Charlotte F., 60
Whaley, Deborah, 39
Whedon, Joss, 124
Wiacek, Bob, 53–55, *54*
Wicca, 22
Williams, Scott, 106, *106*
Windsor-Smith, Barry, 5, 70
Wolfsbane, 13, 83
Wolk, Douglas, 3–4, 7, 10, 79, 111, 130n4 (chap. 2)

Wolverine, 89
Wolverine/Logan: 1982 miniseries, 79–82, *81*; cameo in *Sovereign Seven*, 112, *113*; character development, 40–42; duel with Rogue for leadership of X-Men, 115; establishment of character, 40–41; found family, 41, 104–5; genre shifts for character, 79–82, 89; in "Inferno" storyline, 102; primal versus civilized conflict, 80–82, *81*; relatability, 42; reunification efforts in Dissolution and Rebirth era, 104–5; vulnerability, 8, 41–42; *Watchmen*'s Rorschach and, 41
Wonder Woman, 17

X-bodies, 12–13, 42. *See also* trauma
X-Factor, 89, 101
X-Men: diversity in representation, 116; evolving characters beyond status quo, 115; no. 100 "End of Days," 117; no. 103 "The Goth," 115; "Revolution" storyline, 116–18. See also *Uncanny X-Men (UXM)*

X-Men Annual, no. 12 "Resurrection," 95
X-Men comics: alternate universe, non-canonical storylines, 119; Claremont brought onboard, 25, 28–29; Claremont's return to, 114–15; *God Loves, Man Kills*, 52–53; retroactive continuity additions, 95–96. *See also* characters; families; progressive representation; *Uncanny X-Men*
X-Men films, 111, 115, 122–23
X-Men Forever, 111
X-Men: The Animated Series, 123, 125
X-Men: The End, 111
X-Men: The Movie, 122
X-Men Unlimited, no. 36 "This One's For You!," 118
X-Men video games, 124
X-Treme X-Men, 119

Yu, Lenil Francis, 116, *117*
Yukio, 69–70

Zigarovich, Jolene, 12
Zuckerberg, Jules, 12

ABOUT THE AUTHOR

Photo courtesy of the author

J. Andrew Deman is an associate professor of teaching in the Department of English Language and Literature, St. Jerome's University, and the Eisner Award–winning author of *The Claremont Run: Subverting Gender in the X-Men*.

www.ingramcontent.com/pod-product-compliance
Lightning Source LLC
Chambersburg PA
CBHW071005160426
43193CB00012B/1922